FINDING MY FIRE

SHERI LUX

Finding My Fire

Copyright © 2022 by Sheri Lux. ALL RIGHTS RESERVED. No part of this publication may be reproduced, stored in a retrieval system, or transmitted, in any form or by any means, or used in any manner without written permission of the copyright owner except by a reviewer who may quote brief passages in a review to be printed in a newspaper or magazine, or broadcast on radio or television or social media. For more information, contact the author at info@sherilux.ca.

Lux, Sheri, 1980

Finding My Fire is an autobiography.

First paperback edition: December 2022

ISBN 978-1-7386812-0-4 (Paperback)
ISBN 978-1-7386812-3-5 (Hard Cover)
ISBN 978-1-7386812-1-1 (E-book)
ISBN 978-1-7386812-2-8 (Audiobook)

Photography: Patrick Beaudry, SNAPePHOTO
Creative Director: Logan Smith, Vixel Design

DEDICATION

To my children.

You are my world.

In memory of

your father who loved us to the moon and back.

A butterfly just knows when it's time to emerge from the cocoon.

ACKNOWLEDGEMENTS

It has taken a village, and I have an incredible one. Thank you to everyone who has picked me up and been there for my family, never passing judgement along the way. You know who you are, near and far. You have been our guiding lights.

Thank you to all the First Responders for all that you do. You are heroes who see the wounded sides of society, and your bravery is commendable. Please surround yourself with the right people, seek support when needed, and take the time to put the pieces back together. *Your family needs you.*

FINDING MY FIRE

Note From the Author

This book began as part of my healing process. One day, I started writing, and this story began pouring out of me. I decided to share my journey, heartache and all, in the spirit of helping others. It's not easy to be vulnerable, but I believe there is strength on the other side of our pain if we are brave enough to lean into it.

I have had the opportunity to share my story many times and have been encouraged to write about it as a means to connect with people who may find they are facing similar struggles. I took that advice to heart, and if I can help one person feel less alone, I will have succeeded. I want to help open conversations about topics we often shy away from. There is too much suffering that happens in silence. There is a need to create safe spaces for each other and be able to speak candidly, or else the stigmas attached to mental health will keep people sick with their vices.

I have been through a lot in the last decade, and all the layers of my story have a common theme . . . embarrassment about opening up about what was happening. My healing journey has been a lot of hard work, and I believe it started when I began getting comfortable having uncomfortable conversations, first with myself, then with others. Connections, love, and support are the backbone of healing.

Mother Nature has figured out how to balance the dark with the light. The coal needs the pressure to reveal the diamond, and the seed needs to sit in the dark until it is ready to embrace the light. Transformation happens in the cocoon. Our experiences and lessons help us grow and spread light for one another.

INTRODUCTION

We all have done it at some point. Hid things from people that we were too embarrassed to share. For years, I filled my beautiful spa bathtub with tears, hiding my pain from the world. My affectionate husband had become a shell of himself. I didn't understand why he acted like he loved me one minute and hated me the next. He had changed so much, and I was always on eggshells. The man who used to love and adore me had become unreliable and abusive. He was communicating so little, and I was forced to become a detective in my own home; to try and make sense of the chaos that was becoming the norm.

"Sheri, you have a problem too, you know."

Those words would become ingrained in my mind and go on to change the trajectory of my life. *How dare he!? Didn't he realize the chaos his drinking was causing this family?! I was only the reason we still barely functioned.* But, after going away for my own treatment, I did indeed learn I had a problem, too - a problem of putting my self-worth in the hands of everybody else. I learned I was codependent. This meant I lacked self-love, and my value was directly related to how people treated me. I became a passenger in my own life.

I was married to an RCMP Officer, and it was a confusing time as we struggled to navigate and make sense of these new toxic behaviours happening in our home. We eventually learned that the changes in my husband were symptoms of PTSD, caused by his Operational Stress Injuries (OSI) from fifteen years on the job. This diagnosis introduced our marriage to rehabilitation, intense therapy, and self-awareness as we learned how we were both contributing to the chaos. He was loud with fists, and I was subtle with excessive control.

He had been secretly using alcohol to numb his trauma, and our family suffered as we tried to adjust to the changes. The random outbursts, unexpected rages, holes punched in walls, harsh words, the list goes on. His was a family secret we kept locked behind fake smiles and a seemingly perfect household. Only a select few knew the realities of what went on behind our closed doors. Our marriage hit a new low when I gave him a black eye, and he threatened to have me charged. We were living in a lonely storm of dysfunction, and neither of us knew how we got there.

Eventually, he agreed to rehab, and then he persuaded me to treat my codependency. We were hopeful as the chaos began to subside, and our life started to feel familiar again. There were still struggles and many ups and downs, especially as I began setting boundaries, but now we spoke the same language. We had tools to use, and support systems to call. But slowly, the addiction began taking over again. Then one chilly night in October, he killed himself.

Just like that. He was gone. He left me. He left his kids. *By choice*. I knew his struggles all too well but in so many ways, I felt immensely abandoned. PTSD created a shell out of the man with whom I had built a life. I now had two grief-stricken children to raise on my own and trauma to process. I was forced to look into my children's beautiful eyes and expose the truth that would change their lives. Their anguished sobs still haunt me.

I became a widow at thirty-seven and now understood the deep, guttural fear and sadness accompanying that title. This winding, terrifying path has led me to dark places I never knew existed. I cocooned for a long time in the thick shadows of grief. The years following my husband's death took me down a volatile path of emotions. I wept, raged, made some poor choices, then made better ones, but most importantly, I was both Mom and Dad for our kids.

His death magnified how alone I felt and truly was. I had lost many family members to cancer over the years, including my mother. I was in the middle of my own cancer journey that fateful night my husband took his life. I had been navigating a road of gene testing, surgeries, complications, and reconstruction that spanned across years and provinces. I hid all this from everyone; I was ashamed of what the surgeries had done to my body. I would be the first in my family to outsmart this silent family killer, but I never anticipated I would be doing it alone.

My family has paid the ultimate price of the embarrassment attached to a mental health diagnosis and the shame of feeling emotionally, physically, and spiritually fragmented. In the face of all this tragedy, I have found peace in the form of forgiveness. I poured my pain and sorrow into the healing power of the arts, which I branded into a company, and it gave me the resiliency and hope to move forward. This is the story about who I am, where I came from, and the journey of how I dug deep and *found my fire,* when some days it hurt even to breathe.

CHAPTER 1
<u>MY ROOTS BEGAN IN HUMBOLDT</u>

"You get one more move, and *that's IT!*"

It was 1987, and my mom was fed up. Her round green eyes were fierce and narrow, and she stood facing her husband with her hands on her hips. It wasn't too often that my mom asserted herself, but when she did, my dad listened. It was the late 1980s and many businesses were failing due to interest rate pressures, and our family business in Humboldt had been no exception. Two years prior, Dad had been forced to declare bankruptcy and began taking opportunities as they presented themselves - even if that meant moving his wife and two kids around Saskatchewan. He was determined to get back on his feet to support us, but he had few options with the unstable economy. But that day, my mom was more concerned about what the constant moving was doing to us kids. She wanted us to develop roots somewhere.

My parents grew up in Humboldt and were high school sweethearts in the late 1970s. When mom was seventeen, she found out she was expecting. She was four months pregnant with my older brother at their shotgun wedding, and Dad immediately dropped out of school to work full time in the thriving family business. Mom only finished grade ten before she became a stay-at-home mom. Immediately both my parents focused on building their new family. By the time I came around three years later, we had a very comfortable life as Dad had become a partner in the family business with his father, mother, and brother.

By the time I was five, the business had faced some challenges they could not overcome. When Dad lost the company, he also lost our home - which was a beautiful acreage on the outskirts of Humboldt. I loved the days of living in that home. The earliest memories of my childhood are in that brick bi-level with the swinging basement bar doors my dad and my grandfather made. The neighbours across the street had horses and kittens that my brother and I would always go and play with. My grandparents all lived in Humboldt, and we spent a lot of time playing cards in a haze of smoke around their kitchen tables. That town was full of family, firm roots, the smell of freshly baked bread, and the feeling of warm belly love.

Humboldt's local SJHL Hockey team was the Humboldt Broncos, and we had three players billeted in our basement. One of them became part of the family, and even his parents spent a lot of time around our dinner table. They joined us for meals, and my dad could often be found having a cocktail talking hockey and life with them. On occasion, when my parents needed a night out, these hockey players babysat my brother and me. I remember one of them had the most beautiful girlfriend, who was always at our house. I thought she looked just like Barbie, with her long, wavy, blonde hair. My dad went on to be the best man at their wedding, and their friendship continued to grow over the years.

I finished kindergarten in Humboldt, and the following year, we moved around a lot during the bankruptcy. I attended three different schools in grade one. We lived in Swift Current for three weeks before my dad's new job transferred us to Moose Jaw. We lived there for a few months before we moved to Naicam. We stayed there for just over a year. I don't have many memories of friends or hobbies during these years, as I think I was mostly an anxious mess. Home never really felt like home anymore, as we were constantly uprooted. It was terrifying being the new kid so often. It's probably where part of my codependency stems from - I was always aware of how others saw me and wanted desperately to fit in. If I wasn't born a people pleaser, I certainly learned how to become one.

But that day, as the sun cascaded into our oak kitchen in Naicam, with her hands on her hips, my mom made it clear there were limits to where she was prepared to go with Dad's new ventures. She had reached her tolerance of moving our family around the province. True to her word, we planned for one more move - to the big city of Saskatoon, a place of ample opportunity. This was the city where my dad could rebuild himself while our family had a chance to establish some stability.

I have a clear memory of Mother's Day, 1988. We drove into Saskatoon for the day. We were looking for a place to rent with the idea of completing our final move that summer before my brother and I started school in the fall. We explored the city in our old maroon car with the windows rolled down. The air conditioning wasn't working, and it was a scorching hot day in May. The wind blew my blonde hair all over my face as I struggled to keep it out of my eyes.

We drove past the Dairy Queen on 8th St, and the lineup of people convinced me that I, too, wanted a treat. I begged and pleaded with my dad for an ice cream cone, but he came up with an excuse not to stop. I thought Mother's Day seemed like the perfect reason to enjoy a treat. But he was adamant, and there was no way he was giving in. Mom kept saying she didn't feel like ice cream, and the lineup was too long. I was relentless as I whined and threw a tantrum. Dad started to get mad, so I resorted to pouting in the backseat as I accepted that I wasn't going to win this one. As the years went on, Dad would later tell us that he didn't have $5.00 in his bank account to foot the bill. That killed him, but his fire had already been lit. It didn't take him long to rebuild - he had a work ethic like none I've ever seen.

Dad was a very hard-working, determined man - an entrepreneur at heart, and he had already tasted success with the family business. We had seen rock bottom financially speaking, and it proved to be a motivation for him. He was always thinking on his feet and was a fabulous inventor. A trait he got from his father. There was nothing he couldn't build, fix, or repair. This would come in handy when he began expanding his overhead door business and creating patents for his inventions.

It took Dad six years to build his door company, and by that time, we could relax financially. By year nine, he had made it to the point where we were very comfortable. I remember a particular Saturday morning in grade eleven. I awoke, and as I greeted my parents, my dad informed me he had just sold my old beat-up car to one of his employees. I threw a fit.

"You did WHAT?!?"

I was so mad as I stomped around the kitchen, fumbling for a cup of coffee, trying to ease my mild hangover from the previous night's pit party. Dad was sitting at the honey-coloured kitchen table, doing his morning crossword puzzle, a daily ritual with his black coffee and cigar. He just looked at me out of the corner of his eye with a smirk, and that's when my mom told me to get in the shower because we were going car shopping. Then, just like that, I waltzed into the dealership with my mom and her heavy purse. A day I will never forget.

At this point, my parents were finally done renting and were able to purchase a cute little home nestled in a cul-de-sac in the southeast end of Saskatoon. It was a blue and white four-level split with an unfinished basement.

As the years went on, the basement would get finished into a large bedroom for me. There would be a hot tub room addition that doubled as a gym. It had a back door that led to a backyard oasis full of raspberries and apple trees. The massive wooden deck hosted many BBQs when all the neighbours got together for block parties.

It was a beautiful house, and my mom made it a home with her love of painting and decorating. She loved creating projects. Sometimes I would come home from school, and the wall would be a new colour, with new furniture to match. She had an eye for design and loved making our home feel trendy, elegant, and beautiful.

My parents were finally in a position where they could spoil us with some of the finer things in life. We began going on more family vacations, and Christmases and birthdays became exciting and full of surprises again. But my fondest memory was when Dad would special order the finest cuts of meat and king crab, and we would have a gourmet seafood feast, laugh, and play games into the night. We did that a few times a year.

But growing up, after seeing all the ups and downs with money, I decided I wanted a stable career with a pension when I was older. My dad had an entrepreneurial spirit, but I saw all the emotions that came with that, which looked exhausting. When he retired, he sold his company for top dollar, so you could say he figured it out by the end of his career. I was always mesmerized by his drive but never thought I'd have the desire to follow in those footsteps.

However, in my 30s, I would walk away from my stable career as a middle school teacher when I realized that I also carried the passion for building a business of my own.

CHAPTER 2
MY BEAUTIFUL MOTHER

Mom was a beautiful woman with her big fluffy blonde hair, soft green eyes, and pastel glasses. Her smile was gorgeous. It was so wide, showing off her perfect teeth, and the most infectious giggle always followed. My mom was almost like a girl herself, and she loved to laugh. It was rare to see her without her hair and makeup done, and the only time she wasn't done up was when she was having her morning coffee in her fluffy robe. She took impeccable care of herself and loved to eat healthy and work out. She was a walking ray of sunshine, and I swear my dad fell more in love with her every year.

Mom was the backbone of support in our family, and she was the strong, quiet type. Behind the scenes, she was the one who called the shots. She was my dad's guiding light, and they had a wonderful, solid marriage.

I remember wanting to grow up and have what they had. They were best friends and did everything together. The only time I saw my parents fight was when my dad bought my mom a frypan for their anniversary. Since money was tight then, he thought he was being practical. She was furious. I don't think she talked to him for days. He made up for it years later when he bought her an identical frypan, but this time with a sparkling diamond ring wrapped inside.

My mom was down to earth, but she also liked all the shiny things. When Dad started making money again, he lavished her with jewellery, and she loved every minute of it. She wore beautiful diamond rings on her impeccably manicured fingers, and I remember when she began mixing white and gold rings, which I always thought was unique. This gold and silver theme would become the inspiration behind the branding of my candles. It was a tribute to my mom's elegance.

I don't know why it was, but I instinctively knew my time on earth with her would be cut short. I remember feeling that she wouldn't be around for long. It was awful to feel that way about my mother, but I always had a deep intuition that my time with her would be fleeting.

I honestly don't remember Mom ever really getting mad at me or my brother. Dad would come home from work and be informed which kid needed a talking to. Dad would never really get mad at us, just disappointed, which was worse. We were given a lot of freedom and space to make our mistakes, and there was always open communication in our home. Mom would spend hours with us before bed, discussing our days. She would cuddle up in bed, and we talked about life. She taught us the importance of prayer and gratitude. Mom was very religious, and she had a strong faith. A faith that would take us to church every Sunday.

She was born to be a mother and was really good at it. Mom loved to make crafts and bake buns and had a way of making the house smell amazing. She thrived being a stay-at-home mom. She even ran a daycare when money was tight. I hated coming home after school to a houseful of noisy babies and mischievous toddlers. They would follow me around and want to play with me - my worst nightmare. But Mom seemed to really enjoy it. I know my dad appreciated the extra money it brought in.

Mom had many friends, and they were constantly filling the house with the sounds of laughter as they would sit and visit for hours. I have an early memory of being four years old, and my mom's little sister was visiting. They were sitting around the dark mahogany kitchen table, and when my mom got up to leave the room, my aunt dared me to take a puff of the cigarette in the ashtray.

This was my first memory of peer pressure - taught by my aunt, who teased me until I had no choice. I put my lips on the lipstick-stained filter, took a baby puff and blew it out. It wasn't so bad. So, I took a more extended puff and inhaled as much as possible. I finished the entire cigarette and was pretty proud of myself until the buzz kicked in. Suddenly, my head was throbbing, and I couldn't see straight. I ran as fast as I could to the bathroom to throw up. At that moment, Mom came back into the room, and her eyes narrowed as she silently scolded her baby sister and shook her head in disappointment. My aunt laughed it off and thought it was cute. It was the introduction to my favourite bad habit that I would pick up again in my first year of high school.

My aunt was always at our house. She and Mom were very close. I was drawn to her confidence and willingness to go against the grain. She was fifteen years older than me and really fun and playful. Her loud laugh could fill a room. She had a carefree nature about her and a personality that drew people in. She was a louder, more vibrant version of my mom. Every time she came over, her hair was a different colour, and her makeup was always strong and bold, with nails and jewellery to match. She loved the 1980s era of playfulness.

When I was thirteen, my aunt encouraged me to attend modelling school. There I learned all about hair, makeup, and skincare, and it ended with a professional photoshoot that did wonders for my self-esteem. Around this time, I traded my thick glasses for contacts and fell in love with makeup trends and colouring my hair.

Eventually, I would trade in the drug store hair dye for the salon experience, and my hair got blonder and blonder over the years. I began working out in our home gym and eventually got a membership down the street with my friends. I was committed to working out as I loved how it made me feel and helped with my anxiety. As time went on, my aunt and I would become very close, bonding over workouts, beauty products, healthy recipes, and holistic healing practices.

My mom and her sister had no idea they were both carrying a gene that had been passed down from their father and would be the contributing factor to their early deaths. After my mother's passing, it would take a decade for our family to figure out that the cancer was genetic.

When I got older, my aunt was the one who encouraged me to outsmart my DNA using preventative surgeries. I was in my mid-thirties and just beginning the surgical process when I found myself standing at her burial on a cold day in February. A cruel, stark reminder of what was stacked against me. Thankfully, I was the first in my family to outsmart this family killer, but it came on the heels of many funerals.

CHAPTER 3
CANCER & THE CABIN

In the early 1990s, my parents bought a piece of land near a lake they both loved. It was two hours northwest of Saskatoon, near Spiritwood. This land was full of tall spruce trees and even taller poplar trees. My parents were obsessed with this property, so much so that their friends also started buying lots nearby. My parents had found their place - their second home. Every weekend they made the two-hour trek. At first, it was to cut down trees, and when that was done, they began laying the foundation for what would become our family cabin. My parents, in increments, built everything by hand as they could afford it. During this time, my older brother and I learned independence. We had the house in Saskatoon to ourselves every weekend, and we loved every minute of it.

When I was fourteen years old, my life as I knew it would change. I was in grade nine, and I vividly remember my mom curling over the kitchen counter in agony. She gasped in pain, caught her breath, and then continued with her tasks. I thought nothing of it until months later when my parents sat my brother and me down to talk. They had some devastating news.

Mom had just been diagnosed with Stage 3 Ovarian cancer and was already scheduled for surgery. The silent killer is what this cancer is known as. There are no symptoms, and it is usually too late when they show up. The doctors had given her anywhere from six months to five years to live. Of course, we all hoped the surgery would be successful, but it would only buy us some time. We were told to plan for all scenarios. Just like that, we were on borrowed time with Mom.

It didn't make sense. She looked the same, laughed the same, and still had those beautiful bright green eyes. Now those eyes were riddled with fear. I remember hugging my mom so tight before going to my room. Suddenly, life felt scary, and I knew my world was about to change. I laid in bed and cried. My biggest fear was coming true. I felt as if I had been punched in the gut. I sobbed and pleaded with God. *Please don't take my mom.* My mom was my world. She couldn't be dying. Understandably, Dad was a mess. He was emotional, and seeing my parents so helpless was scary. Mom and Dad were only in their mid-thirties.

One of the first things Mom's specialist asked was whether she had a daughter. So, from the age of fourteen, I was constantly checked and prodded by doctors. I was also given birth control, which was thought to decrease my odds of developing cancer.

Mom had her surgery, and two large tumours were removed. I remember sitting in the stark waiting room for what seemed like all day. Finally, the doctor arrived and said the cancer had not spread and that the tumour removal was successful. Mom started chemo soon afterward, and all we could do was hope for the best.

During this time, Mom's father was also diagnosed with cancer. He stayed with us during this time since we lived in the city, and he needed to be close to the treatment centre. So, Mom and Papa would go to the Cancer Centre together to receive their treatments. I loved having my papa at the house. But Papa's battle wasn't very long, and by the end of my grade nine year, he had passed away. That was a tough time for our family. It shook us to the core because Mom wasn't out of the woods yet, so everyone's mind wandered to the unthinkable. Before Papa died, he said he wanted to return as a hummingbird. So that summer, Mom put hummingbird feeders all over her oasis of a yard and, like clockwork, whirring hummingbirds would appear daily. Our comforting reminder that Papa wasn't very far away.

I will never forget the evening when my mom's hair began falling out. She was sitting in her big brown rocking chair in the family room and watching TV. She ran her hands through her curly blonde hair and shrieked. Her trembling palms were holding a clump of hair. Wide-eyed in disbelief, she started panicking, gasping, and pulling out more. I was speechless because, up until that moment, she seemed fine. I ran over to her and didn't know what to say or do. I just looked at her, and tears started coming down my face. Cancer was visible right there in front of us for the first time.

Mom underwent vigorous rounds of chemo treatments that would make her very sick. I remember her losing her appetite, and she always felt flu-like. She had had more bad days than good days for almost a year, but she still looked amazing and trendy with the cutest wigs and scarves.

Mom's nine months of chemo treatments were a success. Our prayers were answered, and Mom officially went into remission. We didn't know how long this remission would last, and she had to get her blood counts tested every three months. I learned so much about white blood counts and CA125 and became obsessed with these quarterly appointments. Whenever her counts were fine, I felt like I had gained three more months with my mom.

She was still as beautiful as ever, with her glowing giggly girl-like spirit. Her hair eventually grew back, and what used to be soft blonde curls were now darker and shorter. I had my mom back, and that was all that mattered. Life could resume. My parents began spending even more time at the cabin, which seemed to be their therapy. They continued to have working bees every weekend, and all the neighbours who were now close friends would pitch in and help each other. My parents were in their glory. They lived for their weekends away. My brother and I did too, but for different reasons. We thoroughly enjoyed converting our family home into a neighbourhood party house.

As siblings, we were pretty close throughout high school, but after my brother graduated, he left to travel across the world. I now had the house to myself when Mom and Dad left for the weekend. I was a free bird. I took advantage of the fact that I didn't have to answer to anyone. I became a social butterfly and loved hosting friends and parties at the house. This went on for years.

Like clockwork, Mom and Dad would pack up the truck and leave every Friday, and my friends would start to trickle in. Sometimes the whole neighbourhood would find their way to our house - and there were plenty of nights when things got out of hand. The parties became louder and bigger and more destructive. It was the Grunge Era. Nine Inch Nails, Nirvana, Snoop Dogg, Offspring, and Alannis Morisette could be heard vibrating through the walls. Our family home was routinely filled with a mosaic of plaid, tank tops, and ripped jeans.

Eventually, I had my final run-in with the neighbours. They were fed up with all the noise and the disruption. One morning they were doing yard work, waiting for me to come outside so they could talk to me. They called me over. I was sheepish. I knew what they were going to say. I had pushed my luck. They had been patient and kind and kept me out of trouble over the years. But even I knew enough was enough.

Then my dad sat me down and told me he knew about the parties and that if I didn't cut it out, they would drag me to the cabin, and I would spend my weekends building and cleaning. The thought of that was punishment enough. The house calmed down after that. I behaved. I was finishing grade twelve now, and the novelty of freedom had worn off. I was still a social butterfly, but I kept the house relatively empty after that (most of the time).

I graduated high school in 1998, and the next thing I knew, I was enrolled at the University of Saskatchewan, working on my English degree and planning to become a teacher. Around this time my mom's cancer came back. It had now moved to her liver. She had more surgery and went back into remission. This was always a stressful time, as we never knew what the cancer would do, and she was already on borrowed time as she had outlived the five-year statistic.

I lived at home until the early 2000s, when my

best friend, Rhonda, dragged me to Lethbridge to breathe new life into me. This is where I met Mike, and the course of my life would change again.

CHAPTER 4
LETHBRIDGE IS CALLING

I had been stuck in a bit of a rut during the first few years of University in Saskatoon. Life felt mundane living at home with Mom and Dad. I hadn't met many new people and was looking for a change. In my second year of university, when Mom and Dad left for the winter to try the snowbird lifestyle, I started partying hard - every night. I was hanging out at the clubs and began hanging out after hours, as some friends knew the owners. The experience was eye-opening to me, and although it was a lot of fun, the initial excitement began to feel routine and hollow. I was ready for a change in my life, but I wasn't sure what that would be.

An opportunity fell into my lap after my third year of university. It was the summer of 2001, and my friend Rhonda was back in town. The year before, she had moved to Lethbridge to attend the community college, and she loved every minute of it. She knew how unhappy I was in Saskatoon and tried to convince me to move to Lethbridge with her in the fall. It was only a few weeks until school started, and I was already enrolled at the U of S. It was too late to make the fall enrolment at the University of Lethbridge, so it didn't make sense. But I knew this move could be the way out I was looking for.

I remember sitting with my best friend's mom, stressing about what to do. I didn't know what my parents would think about this move. We decided the best option would be to write my parents a letter. That way, they could digest it, and I would have time to prepare my argument. I thought for sure this would be a fight. So, I penned a letter and left it on the hall table.

When I came home, my parents were thrilled at what they had read. They agreed that it was time for some changes for me. So, within days, I packed up what would fit in my silver sports car, and Rhonda and I were off on what would be the exciting start of my next life chapter.

We moved into a dingy apartment that had fake grass for carpet. It was the most ridiculous one-inch-long horrible green carpet we had ever seen. We needed a lawn mower instead of a vacuum. But we loved that place and took any furniture anyone would give us. We had mismatched love seats and a trunk for a coffee table. We had just enough dishes to make it work. We loved sharing clothes, hitting the gym, and curling up and watching old movies after cooking a gourmet meal of Kraft Dinner. We had a lot of fun living together that year.

Rhonda was a showstopper with gorgeous ice blue eyes, wavy mahogany hair, and her laid-back, carefree personality. We would blast Eminem, Britney Spears, and Destiny's Child, pour drinks and get ready for hours before hitting the clubs. We typically ended the night with my late-night buttery perogies. These became a staple in our home.

I worked a casual job waitressing at a nearby restaurant. My mom's little sister lived in Lethbridge, and was just as fun as ever. I would run into her at the nightclubs every once in a while - Roadhouse and Caddie's were the fast favourites. We were similar free spirits who enjoyed having a good time and loved to laugh.

Not long after we moved to Lethbridge, I got the news that Mom's cancer had returned … again. Her cell count came back high. I went into panic mode. I was so glad to have Rhonda there; she was my rock and loved my mom like her own. She was a blessing during this time, as she could calm my anxiety.

Over the next four years, Mom would do her treatments and go in and out of remission. Her body would be riddled with countless surgeries, and she began taking medication to counteract the hair loss and other side effects. But this began to take a toll on her body, and her quality of life became affected. The treatment seemed as bad as the cure. It became apparent that we were now on significantly borrowed time with Mom.

CHAPTER 5
THE NIGHT I MET MIKE

I had been living in Lethbridge for two months when Rhonda insisted I try to meet someone. She promised this was the last man she would introduce me to. She knew so many people from her time in Lethbridge, and she had been trying to set me up with numerous bachelors since we moved there. And, to be honest, I was sick of it. I was enjoying my freedom and all the unknowns of being single. But this particular night in October, I agreed to meet this one man she was insistent on. I was tipsy in a dimly lit nightclub, and the course of my life would forever be changed.

"You have to come and meet him *NOW!!*" Rhonda frantically pulled my hand and began dragging me across the bar. I struggled to keep up with her in my knee-high boots and long black skirt with a thigh-high slit. She told me she had just talked to him and convinced him to meet me, and she wanted to get me over there before he changed his mind.

Whoa!! . . . What? Who did this guy think he was? No way. If she had to convince him, I wasn't interested . . . well . . . maybe a bit intrigued. But there was no way I was rushing over there.

I released my hand from hers. I decided I would meet him, but he could wait. I went to the bar, chatted with some friends, refilled my drink, and then I remember grabbing a cowboy hat off someone's head and sauntering over to this mystery man who had granted me a meet and greet. *As if!*

I swayed up to him without a care in the world, to the beat of Mary J Blige thinking, *here we go again, Rhonda,* but then our eyes locked, and time stopped. I met Mike.

We had an instant, inexplicable deep connection. We were in a loud and noisy bar, and we found a quiet table at the back and talked all night. There was something about him that instantly felt like *home.* He was so funny and yet had so much swag. He was so . . . intimidating. Few men intimidated me, but I was drawn to this man who gave no one the time of day. Yet he couldn't take his eyes off me. I was used to getting attention in the clubs, but he looked at me differently. He actually *saw* me. We laughed; he teased me and spun me on the dance floor. He was an awful dancer, but the way he poked fun at himself was so cute. He had an energy that I wanted more of.

That night he made me feel like I was the only person in the world. We went back to my dingy apartment for my famous buttery perogies and chatted all night. After our bellies were full, we fell asleep mid-conversation on the floor, leaning against the faded grey loveseat. I woke in the morning to what would become a memorable story at our wedding and again at his funeral.

When I woke up, I found myself alone in the living room, as Mike was nowhere to be found. I was bummed. We had had such a great time together, and now he was just . . . *gone*. A million thoughts went through my head.

My insecurities flared because I liked him and was shocked he wasn't there. I was moping around, and then to my surprise, when I went into the bathroom, I found a piece of toilet paper attached to the wall with Band-Aids.

It was a hideous sight - a thin, torn piece of toilet paper covered with barely legible writing. It looked like a three-year-old was learning to write. The wrappers from the Band-Aids were still littered on the vanity and the floor. I cocked my head from side to side as I assessed the scene. A slow smile crept over my face. It had Mike's name and phone number written in blue pen. The rest is history. It was the start of Mike's romantic endeavors as he spent the next few years sweeping me off my feet.

I floated into Rhonda's room and laid in bed with

her as we recapped the previous night. I was nervous and excited to see where this new relationship would go. I called him later that day, and we talked for hours. We began spending more and more time together, and I didn't know what it was about him, but he just felt like a missing piece of my life that I didn't realize I was missing. Everything was just so easy with Mike.

One thing led to another, and a few dates later, he invited my friends and me to Fernie for New Year's Eve. So, we filled a beautiful townhouse with college shenanigans and had a fun weekend. I don't even think I set foot on the ski hill, or outside for that matter. It was such a fun New Years. So many laughs, new people, and memories. One for the books.

By mid-January, Mike found out he was accepted into Depot; the RCMP training academy in Regina, for a February start. He was ecstatic. He had waited his whole life for this. All he wanted was to be an RCMP officer. I was proud of him but selfishly sad, as I didn't know what that meant for us. I was now in full-time classes at the University in Lethbridge until April, and his training would go into July. I had plans to apply to the College of Education in the fall. So, I was nervous that after our quick start, we would be forced to end things.

I spent as much time as possible with Mike during those last few weeks when we were both still in Lethbridge. Then he moved to Regina for his training with the RCMP. He was so sad to leave me. But, to my delight, we still talked every day. He made a point of emailing love letters every single morning. It was the highlight of my day. That was when I learned about the romantic man I was falling hard for. He was so candid and sweet. We were falling in love, yet I was too scared to admit it to him. He became my best friend. He talked me through my worries about my mom, encouraged me to follow my dreams of one day being a teacher, and reassured me constantly that everything happens for a reason, the way it is supposed to.

He was determined to make our long-distance romance work. We would meet halfway in Swift Current a few times over the next few months. It was about a three-hour drive for each of us. He would tell me about his training and all the new people he met. He was so lit up. It was exciting to see. I finished school in April and moved back in with Mom and Dad until I figured out what my life would look like. Mike drove to Saskatoon every single weekend from April to July. He would work extra hard all week so that he didn't have homework and was able to spend his weekends with me. We grew closer, and he felt more and more like home. I wanted to live my life with him - whatever that looked like.

I remember the very first time my parents met him. Mike arrived in the middle of the night on a Friday. I let him in the house, and he crept into my room. He was nervous about meeting my parents the following day.

In the morning, I got up early to have coffee with my mom and let Mike sleep in, as I knew he would be tired. He would later tell me that when I was upstairs, my German Shepherd named Shadow came in to give him a surprise greeting. Shadow had been in my parent's room when Mike arrived. That morning Mike was greeted face to face with the 100 lb dog pinning him down as Shadow stood directly above him. Mike awoke to Shadow's cold nose on his and tried his best not to panic as this dog cocked his head from side to side, trying to assess who was in my bed.

Mike was not scared of dogs, as he had always owned Rottweilers, but this particular incident had him calling for me to rescue him. If that wasn't bad enough, he then had to walk upstairs and meet my parents for the first time. My dad, loving to have the upper hand in the situation, shook Mike's hand and, to Mike's horror, said, "Well, it's nice to finally meet the man who sneaks into my home in the middle of the night to sleep with my daughter."

As confident as Mike was, he was mortified in that moment, and it was one of the few times I've seen him speechless. I will never forget his nervous laugh; I honestly think that is the only time I have heard it. He managed to charm my dad over, and he and my dad would come to love each other. Mike would be included on snowmobile adventures and hunting trips, and they would build projects together. To my parent's delight, Mike would fall in love with the cabin as we began to create the earliest memories of our life together.

CHAPTER 6
RCMP POSTING IN LA LOCHE

Mike was thriving at Depot. He took his RCMP training very seriously, and I remember him polishing his High Brown boots and Sam Browne belt on the weekends. That was usually the only homework he brought with him. He put so much thought into everything he did. He would grab us some beers, tuck me in with a blanket on my parent's leather sofa, and then start polishing. We would visit and laugh and just enjoy each other's company. I always teased him that the leather looked 'good enough' but, according to him, there was always one more swipe of polish it could use.

It became apparent fairly soon that Mike would excel in his career at a rapid pace. He was driven, focused, and truly loved every minute of the training. Mike was meticulous with details and respected authority, so he had no problem with the grueling training and strict schedule. He loved it. I knew he would make an incredible police officer, and I was so proud of him.

I had just convocated with an English degree, and I was planning on extending my studies to be a teacher. But now I was confused about what to do. Mike and I had been doing long-distance for a few months, and we both hated it. Although we talked every day, and I still woke up to love letter emails, which were still the highlight of my day. The reality was that this long-distance relationship was challenging because I wanted to be around him all the time. He made me laugh and feel safe, and we could talk about anything. There was no place I would rather be than curled up with him. We adored each other. He was incredibly affectionate, always kissing me and giving me big bear hugs, and you would often find my legs draped over his while he rubbed my feet. We fit.

On our weekends together, we would nervously talk about where his first posting could be and what it would mean for us. If he got somewhere within commuting distance, I could still attend school in the city. I felt like my future was in the hands of the RCMP because wherever they posted him directly affected my next decision. We talked about being near Spiritwood, or maybe North Battleford, so we could live at the cabin. My parents were over the moon at this idea.

The day finally came! Mike got his posting! Oh,

how we had waited for this day and were relieved to find out so we could plan accordingly. I thought he was kidding when he told me La Loche. He loved to tease me, so when he said La Loche, I was like, "Haha, okay, where are you really going?" The sad look on his face said it all. I saw the fear in his eyes for what this might mean. He was scared it would be the beginning of the end for us.

He wanted me to come and live six hours north of Saskatoon, where the highway ends, but he didn't expect me to. He realized it was the farthest thing from what we were planning or hoping, and he wasn't sure how we would make this work. He didn't have much time before the move and, in the meantime, he had graduation and a badge to receive. He was busy finishing his training in the early weeks of July 2002. There was a lot of hustle and bustle as all his troop mates were busy exchanging news about their posts and excited and nervous as they were finally about to chase and fulfil their career dreams. They had all worked incredibly hard and had earned every bit of that badge. I was so proud of him, but selfishly I was sad. It felt so bittersweet.

A few days after his grad, it hit me. I had to go with him. There was no question. We had just done six months of long-distance and were only two hours apart. There was no way in hell I was going to be six hours from him for weeks on end. It just wasn't an option. He was relieved when I told him. He never hid the fact that he wanted me to move with him, but he didn't want to be the reason I didn't have the career I desired. He worried my parents would be disappointed and didn't want to wear that hat.

But oddly, my parents were excited for me when I told them. They loved Mike and saw how he treated me and how miserable I was when we were separated. So just like that, after his grad, he packed up and started prepping for his big move. He went up a week before me to get sorted out. He had a ton of unknowns facing him at the end of that six-hour drive.

He called me the first night and was a little quiet. He knew I wouldn't be happy living in such a small, isolated community full of stray dogs. It was one of the roughest postings in Canada, known for its high crime and poverty, and most locals lived off government assistance. He braced me, but nothing could have prepared me for the drive.

My parents drove me up, and we took two vehicles packed full of my life. I was nervous about embarking on this new adventure. The highway took us past Battleford, near our cabin, so that part of the drive was familiar. However, the farther north we went, the more potholes we dodged. The towns became fewer and farther between. We drove through a little town called Buffalo Narrows, and we only had an hour to go. But something seemed to change. The energy shifted on the highway, and suddenly there were diapers in the ditches and stray dogs everywhere. They were the oddest-looking dogs, too. Small, like Dachshunds, but with big heads, like German Shepherds. We couldn't help but stare, but we weren't sure what we were looking at. They were a hideous sight and are burned in my memory to this day.

What unsettled me the most was the bullet hole in the town sign. The bullet hole itself was unnerving, but the fact that it was in the silhouette of the Mountie's head really caught me off guard. Thick tears welled up. I immediately changed my mind. I told my parents that I didn't want to do this anymore. I wanted to go home. But it was too late for that.

I pulled myself together, and we soon followed Mike's handwritten directions. Two right turns later, we eventually found my new home in the shape of a bland ivory-coloured duplex.

Mike opened the door as we pulled up. He had taken some time off work to be home to greet us. He was on duty and wearing his uniform. He looked so handsome. That was the first time I had seen him as an official police officer with a radio and all the devices on his belt. He looked like he had been doing the job for years. All I could think about was how surreal it was to see him finally living his dream career, and all he could think about was what I thought about this town I would now call home. He was nervous about what my parents thought of him dragging me up here. But, honestly, seeing him so professional and how he greeted me put everyone's mind at ease. This was where I was supposed to be.

After ensuring we had what we needed, Mike returned to the detachment on the other side of the chain-link fence in our new backyard. He had a couple more hours left on his shift, but he told us he would pop in and out. My dad began unloading the truck, and we walked around the house. It was a simple three-bedroom bi-level with an unfinished basement.

That basement would go on to host many parties, including two years' worth of RCMP Christmas potlucks. It would be strung with Christmas lights and lawn chairs as we laughed and did silly gift exchange games into the wee hours.

But that hot August day, as we began unpacking the vehicles, I was getting increasingly excited about what this all meant. Mike and I were finally done living long-distance, and even though this posting changed many of my plans, I just knew everything was going to be okay.

Within the first few days, I met all the RCMP members and their partners. They held a welcoming party for us. I was nervous about going, as I didn't know what to expect, yet I knew these people would be my lifeline. It was a relief to discover we were all around the same age and in the same stage of starting our adult lives. Some of the women were nurses; some were teachers. Many were in brand new relationships just like Mike and me. Everyone was so friendly and welcoming, and I immediately hit it off with a few of the girls. It was fun meeting all these police officers that were full of life and felt invincible. Most were rookie cops, just like Mike, with freshly earned badges. This was when we met some people who would play a key role in our lives later on. Morgan, Greg, and Zena would become part of our inner tribe years later when Mike's PTSD from working in this northern community would begin to bubble up.

Within the first week of moving up there, Mike had found me a job. It was at the local gas station/store/bank. I got all dressed up to meet my new boss. I was so nervous. I drove the six blocks to the location as it felt safer than walking. That alone tells you everything you need to know about the town. When I got there, a big burly man with a thick grey beard greeted me. He looked like a lumberjack and had a prominent booming voice that matched. Ron was a sweetheart. He had a heart of gold and loved to tell stories and laugh.

I had a desk in the back room, right beside his. My job was to do paperwork and cash cheques and help keep things running smoothly. The only thing that made me a little queasy was all the exotic animal heads staring down at me. Ron was so proud of them. I got to know him quite well, and he told me all the stories behind each one. He and his son alternated spending time up north running the store. They typically only employed Mountie spouses, so they were generous with days off. It was just a given that when Mike had his week off (every six weeks or so), we would go down south to visit friends and family. Ron and my dad hit it off when my parents came to visit. My dad designed an electric gate for his compound, then did maintenance on all the garage doors at the RCMP detachment. My parents were always looking for excuses to come back and visit.

While living in La Loche, we decided to get our first dog. Mike had always had Rottweilers, and although I wanted a German Shepherd, he won this particular standoff. We picked out a beautiful puppy from breeders in Porcupine Plain. Mike loved this dog, which we named Desna. She was treated like a baby; she became our focus as she took over our bed and home. She didn't have much time to enjoy her special status before she got demoted when our baby arrived. But we loved her, and although she was a lot of work and always got into trouble, we gave her a good life. Mike had peace of mind knowing I was home with a large dog. I also felt more protected when he was gone.

During his downtime, Mike loved to spend time in nature, and we would always take Desna to the lake, where she would fetch sticks. We played tricks on her by throwing rocks. She would tucker herself out because she refused to come back without something in her mouth. She would swim in circles looking for the stones. We would have to throw a stick, so she had something to bring back, and then she slept for days. We had to find creative ways to exercise her because we couldn't walk her on a leash in town due to the many stray wild dogs, which were intimidating and unpredictable.

Mike loved the challenges of his first posting. He took much pride in learning the ropes, and all the members gained a lot of experience at this busy detachment. A lot of closeness developed between the officers, and it seemed the more traumatic the calls, the closer they would bond. These members saw a lot in this northern village, including a great deal of violence and gruesome assaults. Their shifts often ended around someone's kitchen table with a bottle of whisky. Alcohol became a standard coping mechanism to process and escape all they had seen.

Looking back, I can see how this time in Mike's career set the groundwork for his PTSD. Eventually, his PTSD would rise up and demand to be dealt with. Back then, we didn't talk about the importance of therapy and being in an isolated community made it difficult to see a therapist regularly and consistently. Alcohol was a quick home remedy to distract and bond through the trauma. To be honest, no one even realized that's what they were doing. It was just a typical way to end a tough shift.

I would get up early to have my morning coffee, and it was not unusual to find my living room full of men finishing their rounds of drinks before heading to their own homes. Our kitchen would be littered with dirty dishes as they feasted on wings, pizza, and whatever they could find in the freezer. Sometimes I would make a lot of leftovers for them to eat, as I knew some of them didn't cook for themselves. In those days, a lot of bonding and discussion happened on our tattered blue hand-me-down couches. Then, they would do it all over again the next night.

Everyone worked hard and partied even harder. Sometimes, after their shift, the guys would join the get-togethers we ladies took turns hosting. The dining tables were always full of homemade dips and cocktails. Everyone got along so well and needed to let loose, but it was always more fun when the men could join in. There was a ton of laughter and banter.

We were all very naïve, for as carefree as life seemed, these members were absorbing and internalizing trauma after trauma, not realizing how deeply it affected them. These experiences came back to torture many of the officers who, years later, admitted they had struggled with their flashbacks and addictions. Mike's funeral was when a lot of them opened up about this. Looking back, we all realized that no one really processed anything properly; it was all smoke and mirrors. Most officers subscribed to the idea that they would be in and out of the posting in two years, using booze, banter, and sarcasm to overcome the tough stuff.

Many of us had come to La Loche as girlfriends, and most left with rings on our fingers. After we all went our separate ways, we continued to visit and spend time with each other. As the years went on, we reunited at weddings, and all the northern shenanigans and memories would come flooding back. The drinks would be flowing, and the stories would be told. The wedding season went on for a couple of years. Eventually, kids began being added to the equation, and not only did we keep in touch, but we also began planning family holidays together.

We also spent a lot of time with my parents those first couple of years in La Loche. They often came up north and never missed one of our seasonal parties. It was great that my parents came up as much as they did, as it was becoming more apparent that Mom was on borrowed time, but I tried not to think about that too much. She still had regular checkups, and her numbers would slowly creep up, but nothing to be alarmed about. I always had an unsettled feeling that my time with her was getting shorter and shorter.

I spent as much time with her on the phone as possible, and since Dad was doing work up in La Loche, she would sometimes stay for a week at a time. She would fill our freezer with homemade soups and meals, and Mike adored having her stay with us.

Mike and Mom got along so well. They had an easy-going understanding of each other. They were both a little on the quiet side compared to my dad and me, and if I was ever frustrated with Mike, my mom was always quick to defend him. Looking back, I am so grateful that Mike had those stretches of time with my mom because, when she passed away, he was able to share the depths of my grief. She was such a beautiful woman inside and out, and the weeks she spent with us really helped them bond.

CHAPTER 7
OUR DAUGHTER

We had been living in La Loche for a few months when I was having lunch with a girlfriend in Saskatoon. We were on our week off, and we always went to Saskatoon, Regina, or the cabin. This particular time Mike went to Regina to spend time with his family, and I stayed in Saskatoon to spend time with some friends.

Jolene was one of my best friends. She was in a brand-new relationship, and we had a ton to catch up on. She met me for lunch at one of our favourite restaurants, and halfway through our conversation, a realization hit me like a ton of bricks.

"Jolene!" I said panicking. "We have to go. We have to leave right now!" My mind began racing. I suddenly realized my body felt different and instinctively knew what I needed to confirm.

"We have to stop at Shoppers." My mind was spiraling a million miles a minute. I couldn't even think straight, let alone put together a proper sentence. "I think I'm pregnant." I blurted it out before I had a chance to stop myself.

"Huh?" she asked with a confused look on her face as her big blue eyes furrowed, her fork raised to her mouth. "No, you're not." She swirled her fork in a circle in midair and continued eating her salad.

"Jolene! It just hit me, my boobs are sore, and my pants are tight, and I don't know when my last period was."

I had been on birth control forever at this point and honestly didn't even think my body worked properly anymore. I didn't even think I'd be able to have kids. But I was late and knew what I needed to do.

I felt nervous. Mike was in Regina, but there was no way I could wait to see him before taking a pregnancy test.

"We need to leave NOW." I threw money on the table, and we were off.

We stopped at Shoppers and went back to my parent's house. Jolene eagerly waited outside the bathroom door.

The results came immediately. There was no question. TWO Lines!!! Oh My God!! My hands were shaking. I was too young to be a mom. I didn't know what I was doing. I was only twenty-two. And when La Loche was done, we were hoping to be assigned somewhere

where I could return to school to get my teaching degree. I could barely think straight.

Jolene was elated! My face was buried in her long blonde hair as I accepted her hug and congratulations. I felt like a wet noodle with a brain to match. She was so . . . happy. And I was in complete shock. I told her I loved her but needed time alone to process this.

I needed Mike. I just wanted him with me. Part of me was excited as I put my hand on my bloated belly. My jeans had been tight, which bothered me because I worked out every day. But now it all made sense. I was going to be a mom. *Holy shit.*

I took Shadow for a long meditative walk, still in disbelief. Then I called Mike. I was shaking. This was not how I pictured making this kind of announcement. I felt like a teenager hiding in my parent's basement. I called his parent's house, and his mom answered the phone. I pretended like I didn't have a million other things on my mind. Thankfully it was a brief catch-up.

When Mike got on the phone, I told him he needed to go into the other room and sit down as I had some news. When I told him, he was ecstatic. He was so excited, and he kept asking if I was sure. He promised not to tell anyone until we had had a chance to digest what it all meant. He immediately came to Saskatoon, and, just like that, all was well in the world.

The next day, we went to the doctor, who immediately sent me for an ultrasound since I wasn't sure how far along I was. That's when we saw our baby and learned our due date was the end of October. I was twelve weeks pregnant. *I was already in my second trimester!* We were having a baby, and it was coming sooner than we thought. It was hard not to get excited around Mike. He was on cloud nine. When we told our parents, they were shocked but excited. This was the first grandchild on Mike's side of the family, and the second on mine, as my brother and his wife had their first child two years prior. As my belly grew, so did my excitement. *I was having a baby!*

    We went back to La Loche but were back and forth to Saskatoon a lot. We coordinated our doctor appointments with Mike's time off. He never missed one. When we were in Saskatoon, Mike and I would spend our days shopping for baby clothes, and I was busy buying and reading books on all the changes my body was undergoing. It had been a really easy pregnancy, and I felt great. I barely skipped a beat. We got the baby's room ready, Mike assembled the cherrywood crib and the change table, and I decorated the room in neutral shades. We didn't learn the sex of our baby by choice, as Mike wanted it to be a surprise. But it killed me not being able to plan!

    I continued to work in La Loche and began training Zena at the store. Her husband had recently been posted in La Loche. She was going to take over for me once I had the baby. I had everything in order, and in late September, it was time to make the transition to Saskatoon. I moved back into my basement bedroom, and Mike finished up his last few weeks in La Loche as we eagerly waited to become new parents.

Mike had been banking time, so we knew that when the baby came, we could stay at my parent's place for a few weeks before heading back up north as a family of three.

Mom and I bonded over the tiny baby clothes. I loved washing and folding them. They represented so much potential. A little person - *my* little person, was going to be wearing them. I was going to be responsible for another human being. It was hard to wrap my head around it. I was in a full-blown nesting phase and loved every minute of it.

I had been in Saskatoon for about a week when I started getting contractions. I called Mike in La Loche, and he was at my parents' house within eight hours, officially on his parental leave. The contractions turned out to be false, and we patiently waited another week before our beautiful daughter arrived.

It was a beautiful sunny Tuesday, and we planned to have a nice dinner and a cozy night watching a movie. We were snuggling on my parent's leather couch when my water broke halfway through *Gangs of New York*. We arrived at the hospital, were admitted, and three hours later, before I could even get pain medication, I was told it was time.

"What?! Nooooooo, I want meds!!"

I refused to deliver this baby without some sort of a painkiller, and I was at a standoff with the doctor. But my body had other plans, and it was time. Within twenty minutes, I delivered a perfectly healthy baby girl.

Mike started crying. *Something I was about to learn he did at all the things that made his heart warm and fuzzy.* I was in awe. She was perfect with her little nose, round face, and healthy cry. She had her dad's piercing blue eyes and perfect little round lips. She looked like something out of a magazine.

We returned to Mom and Dad's house with our little pink bundle, just in time to show her off for Thanksgiving. She was the most beautiful baby. She loved to sleep from the day she was born, a trait she has never outgrown.

She was a dream for a first-time mother. She cuddled whoever was holding her and smiled all the time. She barely ever cried, and sometimes I even had to wake her up to feed her. No one could get enough of her. My parents loved having us at the house, and my mom absolutely adored her. This little girl was Mike's pride and joy, and he was the most protective father. We were officially a family.

CHAPTER 8
<u>FINALLY...HE PROPOSED!</u>

Mike and I weren't engaged, and it started bothering me. As my belly began to swell with my pregnancy, so did my resentment at not having a ring on my finger. We spent countless hours sharing our dreams and plans. We knew we were going to get married, so I couldn't understand why he wouldn't ask me officially.

Every time we travelled down south, I would try on engagement rings and ask the salesperson to write down the information on a card. I began bringing these cards home and casually passed them to Mike. They had all the information he needed, including ring size, location, and price. Then I started to be less subtle about it. Eventually, this went on long enough that I began to pick fights with him over it. When I look back, and if I'm being honest, my feelings were hurt. I didn't understand why he would withhold something I wanted so badly. "Be patient" was all he would say. Patience is not a virtue I was blessed with.

Every time we would get dressed up, go out for dinner, or head to the mountains, I would think *tonight is the night,* only to be disappointed. I remember on my birthday, when I was about five months pregnant, Mike made dinner and hotel reservations for us in Saskatoon. I got my gel nails done the day before and chose a pretty shade of pale pink. I wanted my hands to be flawless when showing off the ring I anticipated receiving within hours. I knew Mike must have been calculating the exact moment. He liked to plan, and he paid attention to small details. I was expecting this beautiful event to be on one of these evenings when I was wearing my expensive leather jacket, and Mike was wearing his favourite cologne.

So, naturally, on my birthday, after he told me he had made reservations at my favourite steakhouse and we were going to spend the evening downtown, I just knew this was the moment I had been waiting for. I took the time to ensure my makeup was impeccable, my hair was curled in beachy blonde waves, and I had the perfect heels. I was ready with my strategic manicure and just hoped I could act surprised enough not to let him know I was onto him. I was going to wake up tomorrow an engaged woman! I couldn't wait.

We had the most amazing candle-lit dinner in a

quiet booth in the corner of the restaurant. He had requested that specific table. It was romantic, and it meant a lot that he had put in so much effort to pay attention to what I liked. I was secretly hoping he wouldn't pop the question in the restaurant. I didn't want the pressure of a public scene in front of people. To my slight relief, he didn't.

Then we went for a stroll down the riverbank. It was a beautiful evening in June, and my hand felt so right in his. Every time we stopped, he would pull me close, and I would wait for it. But it never came. *He must be waiting until we get to the room.*

We were staying at a hotel on the riverbank in Saskatoon, and when we arrived back at our room, there were no flowers, chocolates, or candles set out as I had imagined. I felt like a decompressed balloon. I washed my face and wiped the silent tears down the drain.

I put on some comfortable clothes, and with my legs draped over his knees, we spent the night talking about life, the baby, what our future would look like, and where we would want to be posted after La Loche. He was rubbing my feet, as he always did. I remember sitting there, and my stomach was twisting and heavy. I knew there was not going to be a proposal that night.

I rolled onto my side in bed and let the hot tears melt into my pillow. I was really hurt, but I was mad at myself for building it up in my head. My head started spinning with all the what-ifs. I began to pull back after that. Maybe this was the universe telling me there was someone else for me. But as I wrapped my arms around my swollen belly, I knew it was just my anger talking. I couldn't see myself with anyone else, and I didn't want anyone else.

    I woke up with a heavy heart when we packed our suitcases the following morning, but I hid my feelings. I became the queen of smiles while feeling despair. I would discreetly lock myself in the bathroom and cry silent tears in the mirror. Then I would breathe deep, wipe my cheeks, and reappear all happy and carefree. This proved to be a codependency trait I wasn't aware of. It was a trait that would be re-played over and over in the next decade. Rejection was the trigger, and it would be in full swing by my mid-thirties.

    Our friends were beginning to get engaged, and wedding fever was everywhere. I was jealous as I fawned and gushed over their shimmering diamonds and elegant wedding plans. I was happy for them, but it magnified the fact that I wasn't making the same plans, yet I was the one carrying a child. I bounced between feeling embarrassed and hurt.

    I started to wonder if Mike even wanted to marry me. Maybe he didn't. Perhaps he thought he did, or sometimes did, but wasn't sure enough to officially commit. I didn't bug him about it anymore. He did all the right things in every other way. At this point, I let it go and stopped creating fantasies in my head. I knew that

I would eventually have to give him an ultimatum down the road because I wasn't going to be his girlfriend forever. I wanted the security of commitment.

Back up north, we settled into our routines, and time went on. I was still working, and I started not to overthink the fact that we weren't planning a wedding before the baby arrived. It was easy to forget about it when we were back in La Loche as the baby started kicking, and I redirected my focus.

I was nine months pregnant, shopping with my mom in Saskatoon, and the sparkle of a jewellery store caught my eye. I went in and was at the enclosed back counter before I knew it. There it was. I'd found *the perfect* ring, and it was on sale. I didn't know what to do. I hadn't mentioned an engagement ring in months and told myself I wouldn't. But all the same, I requested the written information and put the card in my purse.

Mom and I eventually finished our shopping and made our way back home. We arrived home to find Dad and Mike preparing dinner. Dad was bustling in the kitchen, concocting the perfect marinade for the tenderloin steaks. Mike was keeping him company, and they were chatting about everything they loved - hunting trips, snowmobiles, etc. Mike was relaxed, and flopped out on the sofa with his arm outstretched across the back. I couldn't resist. I gingerly put the card on his knee and walked away. No words were exchanged, but my turquoise eyes said it all. He came up and gave me one of his big bear hugs, kissed me all over my face, and then called me a spoiled brat. Once again, he told me to be patient. I rolled my eyes, and that was the end of it.

Mike had a reprieve from talk of an engagement once the baby arrived. I was so busy discovering how to be a new young mom that nothing else mattered. There were so many things to learn about this little baby and the changes happening to my body. I forgot about the ring and all it represented during this time. I had a new, more important focus - this tiny human who relied on me for everything. It was the best feeling in the world.

After spending those first weeks as a family of three in Saskatoon, we arrived back in La Loche late at night on a cold November evening. Mike took the baby into the house and told me he would deal with the rambunctious dog and the overfilled truck. He wanted me to get settled and said he would worry about the rest.

He was adamant that he didn't want help and just wanted me to get tucked in and look after the baby. So, I threw on my old grey sweats and took the baby to bed with me to feed her while Mike unloaded the truck.

I was exhausted, and sleep began to wash over me. Our daughter was nestled in the curve of my side, and she had fallen asleep while feeding. It was my favourite part of motherhood so far. The rawness of my body doing what it was made to do. It was sustaining a new life, and the whole meaning of what that meant washed over me. I wondered if my mom had also felt this way when she was a new mother in the 1970s. I started thinking of my mom at my age, and it made me feel differently toward her. I didn't think I could love her any more, but thinking about the generations of family made me realize how precious life truly is. Life was making a full circle. I felt connected to both my daughter and mother as my thoughts pushed and pulled through the past and the future. I now understood. *This is how it feels to be a mom - so much love.* I basked in that moment as my sleepy eyes took in every inch of her peaceful little face.

    Mike poked his head in at us, and I asked him if he would take her to her bassinet. As he reached to pick her up, I couldn't help but admire the way he looked at her. It was a deep love that went beyond fatherhood, and I knew it gave him a sense of pride and purpose. He just exuded and radiated light in her presence. Their connection was incredibly strong from day one.

    As he scooped up our sleeping baby and took her to her room across the hall, I can still remember his deep voice as he lifted her out of my arms. He murmured so softly and was so gentle. I rolled over with a smile and let a deep feeling of contentment wash over me. We were home, and I was in my cozy bed. Life felt good. I was basking in this warm feeling of gratitude when Mike very quickly interrupted that.

    He bellowed my name in a panic from across the hall. He started making gagging noises. *Oh Mike, you need to get used to this.* This was becoming a routine. He had a sensitive stomach and always required me to take over when it came to diapers. Just like that, I was shaken from my peaceful sleep to go and help a grown man deal with the basics of fatherhood.

Seriously Mike. You're a police officer! Can't you change a diaper on your own? I begrudgingly pulled myself out of my warm bed and adjusted my old U of S sweats that were sliding down my hips, as the elastic band was worn and tattered. My blonde hair was barely encased in a messy ponytail, and my hands fumbled to find my glasses that had slipped off the nightstand. I was tired and groggy as I slumped across the hall. *Jeeez Mike*. Our baby was on the change table when I entered the room, and Mike was hovering next to her.

Robotically, I began undoing the buttons on her pink and white striped sleeper. Her little legs started kicking, and her eyes lit up when she saw me. Despite feeling tired, I couldn't help but smile at my tiny little girl. Her breathing got fast as she cooed, telling me she was so excited to see me. My heart was exploding with love for her. I was lost in that feeling and never noticed Mike behind me.

It took me a minute to notice there was something different about her. *Why was she wearing a ribbon?* Mike must have distracted her with one of the many pink balloons floating around the ceiling. I thought nothing of it until I got to the third button on her sleeper, and there it was. *The ring.* The ring I wanted so badly - a perfect

0.75 ct classic solitaire in white gold.

Tears started to prickle in my eyes. I turned around to Mike, who was waiting patiently. He got down on one knee and said the most beautiful things to me. He was crying as he told me what I meant to him and how his life was finally making sense. He told me he'd needed me to be patient, not because he wasn't sure about us, but because he wanted *me* to be sure this was what I wanted. He said he was waiting for the perfect moment and didn't want me to get caught up in all the superficial fluff. It was so raw and romantic. The room was exploding with emotion.

I had envisioned this proposal so many times in my head. The perfect manicures, being dolled up somewhere fancy, but he had managed to catch me off guard completely. I had given up on the notion that he could even surprise me with a proposal because I was always expecting it. But he did, and it changed my perspective on life.

He reminded me about what was really important. This was what life was about. He loved me in a way I had never experienced before and haven't since. The moment did not take place on a mountaintop or at a fancy resort with all the bells and whistles like I thought I wanted. It was just us, in the privacy of our home, with our daughter. That was all that truly mattered.

As frustrated as I had been during my pregnancy, I am so thankful he proposed to me the way he did - I was at my most vulnerable and authentic. I always joked that if he could get down on one knee when I looked as disheveled as I did, he must *REALLY* love me. I thought I looked absolutely dreadful, but that's not what Mike saw.

To this day, the perfection of his proposal is enough to take my breath away. He anchored me. He showed me what mattered, not only in that moment but in life. Mike was always about the simple things. I was always about the shiny things. But we complemented and balanced each other.

I later learned that he had, indeed, asked my father for permission to marry me months before, and he took both my parents to pick up the ring the day before we headed home. It was the same ring Mom and I had chosen earlier that week. The fact that he involved my parents made it feel special, but including our daughter made it feel complete.

CHAPTER 9
THE MOVE TO SASKATOON

We were now engaged, and I was so excited to plan our wedding. But, in the meantime, we still had nine months left up north. This was when our little girl was nicknamed "La Loche Party Baby." We still went to all the potlucks and get-togethers, but we had our little baby doll in tow. Everyone loved her, and she was passed around at parties and would often snuggle into whoever was holding her and fall asleep. She was a social butterfly from the get-go. She loved people, and the noise didn't bother her.

    We were pretty laid-back parents, me more so than Mike. But we were a good balance. He loved getting up with her in the middle of the night and was a very hands-on dad. He called her Baby Girl, a nickname she has never outgrown, even since his death. Mike was an incredibly protective partner and father. I sometimes wonder if all the bad stuff he saw at work influenced him to be even more attentive. We were his world, and he took so much pride in taking care of us.

Those last nine months flew by! I really appreciated Zena during this time, as she would be taking over my job when we moved away. She and her husband had two kids, and it was nice to connect with another mother. Zena was a godsend, and Mike thoroughly enjoyed his shifts with her husband. He also appreciated being able to talk with someone who knew about parenting.

But, for now, our countdown was on, and we were eager to find out where our next posting would be! We had put in our request. We wanted any sort of city, but after being up north, we would have been happy with a large town. We were hoping we'd be close to a university so I could continue my studies.

Mike came home one day absolutely elated! "We got Saskatoon!"

It was our number one choice, and it made our future feel bright and full of promise, as I knew it meant I could eventually go back to school and become a teacher. We were so excited! We called our parents, and everyone was so happy for us. It meant we were going to be closer to all of our family. I immediately went online to begin looking at houses. We were going to buy our first home!! I couldn't wait. We had put some money away for a down payment and were ready for this new chapter.

We looked at many houses during our house-hunting trip in Saskatoon, and it became discouraging. We couldn't find what we were looking for. But then we did. It was a brand-new home at the stage where we could still choose the finishing touches. I thought I had died and gone to heaven.

It never crossed my mind that we could afford a new home. I was one happy girl. I had a wedding to plan *and* a new home to design. The house we found was a bi-level with an unfinished yard and an unfinished basement. It was perfect because Mike and my dad loved to build, and they loved new projects. My mom and I loved to spend money and decorate. So, it was settled. We bought our first home and had a few years of projects to plan and keep us busy.

My parents were so excited to have us return to Saskatoon, especially because we were bringing our little munchkin, who would be a six-minute drive away instead of a six-hour jaunt. I was full of gratitude to be close to my mom again. She was still being checked regularly for cancer, and things hadn't been very good for a while, but they seemed to be okay at the time. I was trying not to focus too much on that because it felt nice to focus on the good things happening for us all.

With the housing settled, we returned north and got ready to say our goodbyes to everyone. There would be a going away party, where everyone would be able to let loose and do something crazy that we would all remember in the years to follow.

It was a time in our life that was full of laughter, and some of my fondest memories of Mike are from this time. He could be Mr. Serious at work, and yet he could be the life of the party after hours. He loved to poke fun and tease, and he could do it in a way that made you like him even more. Mike was in his prime during those years. He was providing for his family and building a career he thrived at and excelled in. He took so much pride in his role as an RCMP Officer and even more pride in his growing family.

CHAPTER 10
<u>OUR HONOUR GUARD WEDDING</u>

A wedding show came to Saskatoon, and Mom and I planned a girl's day. We were excited to spend time looking at flowers, tulle, and decorations. We wanted to get some ideas for the upcoming big day. Mike drove down a few days later, and we finalized a few more details, including a photographer we loved. Her portfolio was stunning, and I was excited to book her. And, just like that, we had a wedding day marked on the calendar. October 16, 2004.

Mom and I had been collecting wedding magazines for the past few months, and I had no idea what I wanted in terms of a dress. I knew our wedding was going to be regal, as Mike was going to wear his Regimental Serge, and we were going to have an Honour Guard, as well as a large wedding party. Mom and I visited every bridal boutique in Saskatoon, and I was beginning to panic a bit; I didn't realize I hadn't given myself much time to order a dress. I didn't know they took almost a year to arrive.

But then I found it. The latest design from Alfred Sung had just arrived as part of the new stock. I even remember seeing it in a bridal magazine, as it garnered a two-page spread. The minute I put on that dress, I knew it was the one. I felt absolutely gorgeous. The way it wrapped around my waist and then cascaded into a glitter of beaded satin that extended down the train. I was sold when the saleslady put the crystal-beaded veil in my hair. The dress was undeniably perfect. It fit my body flawlessly, and I didn't want to take it off.

Next, Mike and I chose the location for the reception. It was at a hotel in downtown Saskatoon, right on the river. It was elegant, and they had room to accommodate our guest list of 200 easily. Shortly after that, all the small details began falling into place. My mom's best friend, who had a cake decorating business, offered to make our wedding cake as a gift. She created flowers out of icing that replicated my bouquet and mimicked the beadwork on my dress. It was a beautiful three-tiered cake with cascading white roses that matched my bouquet.

During this time, I remember my mom being more tired than usual. She was still getting her routine bloodwork, and some numbers were creeping up, but she was in the normal range. It was something that was constantly in the back of my mind. But planning the wedding and then the move to Saskatoon kept us all pleasantly distracted and busy.

Mike loved his new position with the Saskatoon detachment. I didn't love it as much, as I worried about him. He often patrolled solo at night, and his backup was rarely nearby. They didn't drive with partners when they patrolled the rural roads around Saskatoon. I missed the number of officers in La Loche. Although it was a small town, many members were posted there, and they were always working together. The sheer numbers gave me peace of mind.

Now that we were in Saskatoon, I often panicked if Mike came home late. Sometimes he couldn't answer his phone or return my call. There were many nights when I would get up with the baby and have an unsettled feeling if he wasn't home.

One night, in particular, he was over six hours late and never answered his phone. I didn't know whom he was patrolling with. I didn't know whom to call. I didn't know what to do, but I managed to convince myself that I would be contacted if there was something to worry about. I remember that night so clearly. I paced and tried to sleep. Cuddled the baby. Repeat. I was sound asleep when Mike got home in the early morning, and he had to wake me up. He looked awful and disheveled, like he hadn't slept in a week.

It turned out he had been in a car accident. He wasn't severely injured, but he had T-boned a car on

Highway 11. He spent the next few hours in the hospital getting assessed, and that's why he couldn't answer his phone. The detachment had wanted to send someone to the house to inform me, but Mike didn't want them waking me up. So, he asked that they just leave me be. When he finally arrived home and reassured me that he was okay, he asked if he had done the right thing. He asked if he should have had one of the guys come to the house.

I told him, sarcastically, that the only time I ever wanted his colleagues to wake me up in the middle of the night was if he was in a body bag. Words that would haunt me over a decade later. My sarcasm that night was something we both shared, and he thought nothing of my comment. He knew me so well that he knew that was how I felt. But that night still replays in my mind. How carefree we were. So nonchalant. We never dreamed that scenario would come to fruition. Memories are funny. I can still feel his hand rubbing my foot as we casually talked about the unthinkable. Yet, thirteen years later, that dreadful knock on the front door is precisely what would wake me.

As the summer leaves slowly began to turn their autumn hues, the details of our big day were all falling into place. The wedding party and the Honour Guard came to Saskatoon a few days before, and we were able to have our bachelor and bachelorette parties and spent some fantastic time catching up with old college and La

Loche friends. Our daughter had her first birthday a week before our wedding, so we hosted a large family gathering. I also had a bridal shower that week - there was so much on the go. It became known as *"Mike and Sheri Week,"* as we kept everyone's schedules full of get-togethers and gatherings.

Finally, our big day arrived. I spent the previous night at Mom and Dad's while Mike and some of the men stayed at our house. The bridesmaids all came to my parent's house at 7 am, and then the limo arrived to take us downtown to get our hair and makeup done. It was a lovely morning of champagne and croissants, mingled with nervous giggles as we all prepped for the day. Once we were back at the house, my dad came downstairs after spending some time with the guys. Mike had a handwritten note for me and had asked my dad to give it to me while I was getting ready.

Mike, the romantic.

My dad presented me with the envelope, and I sat down and read it as a smile crept over my face. It was short and to the point, and it was perfect. Mike was nervous and wanted to remind me that we were just starting to build our life and that we had so many things to look forward to.

This was one of the many love letters Mike had written to me. They started with flirty emails in college, and then when we lived together, I would wake up to handwritten notes by the coffee pot. My birthday cards from him always included handwritten paragraphs. He made me feel like an incredibly loved woman, something I never took for granted. So, this particular morning, I was not shocked to read his note, but it was a beautiful surprise, nonetheless. He was nervous. Not about us, but that our day would go how I wanted it to. He was excited to officially start a life together as a married couple.

Then the moment came when we arrived at the church. I remember beginning my walk down that aisle so clearly. My dad fluffed my six-foot-long train and perfectly positioned my crystal-beaded veil on my shoulders. As we slowly made our way to the front of the church, I saw only Mike. Waiting. Wiping his eyes. I was so engulfed with love at that moment. It was as if nothing in the world could ever go wrong. Those beautiful crystal blue eyes were fixated on me - my *big baby*. I always called him that.

At work, he had a reputation as Mr. Serious - an intimidating man who rarely cracked a smile. He had a deep booming voice and an icy glare no one would mess with. Yet he would melt like putty when he looked at me or his children. We were his weakness. When I walked down the aisle that day, he couldn't hide the tears that rolled down his cheek. He didn't even try.

We said our vows and exchanged rings. We agreed to surprise each other with engravings inside our rings. I couldn't wait to read what he had chosen. He grabbed my face passionately when he kissed me and didn't let go.

I remember his warm hands engulfing my cheeks. His palms felt so strong yet gentle. In one long, romantic kiss, he conveyed it all. That kiss became the talk of our wedding.

Once the formalities were over, we had an enjoyable night dancing and catching up with the guests. So many laughs. So much fun. When we shut it down in the wee hours, we realized a blizzard had rolled in during the night. Flights were cancelled, and roads were closed. We were supposed to drive to Jasper for our honeymoon, but instead, we basically hosted a frat party for a few days. Many people were stranded, and we had the spare room in our home. So, the party continued for days at our house. We never did take a honeymoon. In fact, our first trip would be to Vegas for our fifth wedding anniversary.

When things began to settle down, and people returned home, I began to have a sick feeling about Mom. I remember her being tired at the wedding. I called her a few days later to see how she was doing, and that call marked the beginning of a long, helpless journey for our family. We would return to that same church in eighteen months for her funeral. Things for me would never be the same after that.

CHAPTER 11
THE LOSS OF MY MOM & OUR BABY

Mom's most recent results arrived a few weeks before the wedding, and they weren't good. She didn't want to ruin anything in terms of the wedding, so she and Dad kept this a secret. But now, it was time to face the truth. Her cancer had spread to different organs, including her lymph nodes and liver. She was now facing the worst-case scenario we all prayed wouldn't happen.

Slowly, Mom went downhill for a little over a year. She would lose a little more weight every month and be a little more tired. I begged and pleaded with God. *Please don't take her. Please grant her some sort of miracle.* I spent every waking minute at their house with our daughter. Mike would often stop by on his shift and have dinner with us. It almost felt as if I had never moved out. I wanted to savour every moment I could with her.

About a year after our wedding, while taking care of Mom, I found out I was pregnant. It didn't come as a surprise, but Mom was very sick at this point, making it hard to focus on my health and pregnancy. I didn't have an appetite and hardly put on any weight. In fact, I think I lost weight. I was so sad. All the time. It was such a desperate feeling knowing that Mom was going to die, and there was nothing we could do. I was in a period of deep grief, and all we could do was wait for the inevitable.

As the weeks went on, I became more excited about the baby. The thought of having another little bundle in the house felt right. Mom always asked how I was doing, and she would talk as if she would be around to see the baby. I never knew if she was in denial about her prognosis or was trying to focus on the positive. Our little girl began to get excited about the baby as well, and this new life became our glimmer of hope. I was due in the summer and knew I had time to prepare the nursery and a new room for our daughter.

I met up with my girlfriend Jen and all her bridesmaids during this time. I met Jen when she was an RCMP member in La Loche. She was shopping for a wedding gown for her wedding to Greg that autumn. We went for a beautiful ladies' lunch, and I remember everyone telling me how thin I looked for being three months pregnant. They said I didn't look pregnant and joked that I was thinner than some of them. I secretly wondered if something wasn't right, but recently I'd always had a pit of dread in my stomach, so I couldn't read my body properly anymore.

As Mom's health continued to decline, I was helping to take care of her daily. I would paint her toenails, and we'd watch movies. Our little girl would entertain her with her singing and cuddles. My grandma also moved in to help take care of Mom. We were always surrounded by people stopping by and wanting to help. Grandma always had delicious food on the stove; soup, buns, and baking ready to be served to whomever popped in unannounced.

Then, one day I knew something wasn't right with my body. Nothing about me felt or looked pregnant, and then I started to show symptoms of a miscarriage. Mike took me to the ER, and the ultrasound showed the baby didn't have a heartbeat. I sat there in disbelief as we learned we had lost the baby. I was immediately scheduled for a D & C, and there was little time to process everything. I felt numb, like I was going through the motions. My mom's fate was looming, and now there wouldn't be a new little bundle coming in the summer.

Mike was by my side through all of it, but when I left the hospital a day later, I was very solemn. I was now grieving another loss. I had been in a state of grief for months over Mom, but this made me feel even more hopeless.

I don't think I properly processed what had happened to me. I became hyper-focused on caring for my toddler and my mom. I had no appetite, and I cried all the time. Our little girl was my saving grace. She was a ball of bright light that could put a smile on my face and give me something to focus on. She was always singing and performing for people, and she looked like a Disney Princess in every room she entered. She was such a girly girl who loved having her beautiful auburn hair done and her nails painted. She came by it honestly. She needed me to be her mom, and I took my role much more seriously, knowing the time I had left with my mom was fleeting. Everything about life seemed so temporary all of a sudden.

Six weeks after the miscarriage, my mom succumbed to her fate. She died peacefully in her bed, surrounded by those who loved her. I was holding her hand when she died. She was finally at peace. She was with her dad. Hummingbirds would be travelling in pairs now in the summertime.

We had a beautiful funeral for Mom, complete with a slideshow full of nostalgic memories of a meaningful life lived. It indeed was a celebration of her life. Lots of people attended her funeral, and I was so grateful for all those loved ones whose lives she had touched. Her bubbly, childlike personality was going to be so deeply missed.

During this time, everyone commented on how thin I was, and then they would offer consolations on the loss of the baby. It was a depressing reminder. But we pulled together as a family, and having extended family around for a long period of time made me feel a little better. But eventually, everyone returned to their everyday lives, and our life slowly began to resume again.

Dad stayed in that white and blue family home for two years before he sold it and built a rustic log home on an acreage. It gave him space to have a welding shop, and he felt grounded, being able to spend so much time tending his land. But the energy in our family was different now. It was clear our family had lost its anchor.

I struggled to find joy without my mom. Everything shifted. Mike and I decided not to try for another baby until the summer. I needed to focus on one thing at a time and process everything that had happened within the past year. It all seemed to hit me at once.

I had a period of profound grief. I was different, and I changed that spring. I began having lucid dreams, sometimes to the point that I was paralyzed and heard loud noises. I googled what was happening to me and learned that I was astral travelling. This began my deep dive into spirituality. I was lucky that Mike was open and receptive to these terms and concepts. So was my mom's younger sister. So, we all went on this exploration together. The more open I became to it, the more experiences I would have. It became beautiful, and I always felt like my mom was close by, or at least trying to be.

Then our daughter started surprising us. She began talking to her grandma as if she was right beside her.

I remember one time, a few months after Mom passed, I was bathing her, and she started staring in awe at something behind me.

"Ohhhhh, Mommy!!! Look!" She was staring behind me and pointing, her blue eyes wide like saucers. She was fixated on something over my shoulder. I was spooked as we were home alone. I nervously glanced over my shoulder and, to my relief, saw nothing.

But she was adamant that there was something I needed to see.

"Grandma! Grandma is so pretty, mom!!! She's dancing!!! MOM!!! Looooook!!! She looks like a princess!" She started giggling and was in a complete trance watching over my shoulder. Our daughter would be blessed with many of these mystical visions over the years, and I loved seeing the excitement it brought her. I couldn't help but wonder more and more about the spiritual realm.

My interests began to change after this, and my old self slowly broke away. I became interested in crystals, angels, guides, meditation, and holistic healing. I questioned religion as I knew it, and my fascination with spirituality increased. However, I felt uncomfortable talking about it with most people. I could sense their energy shift when they started looking at me differently. I learned very quickly to keep much of this to myself or only to share with Mike and a few friends.

But something awakened in me, and I knew I wanted to explore it more. In time, I would.

CHAPTER 12
OUR SON

Two months after Mom's funeral, the night before Mother's Day, I woke up in the middle of the night and couldn't fall back asleep. I had a vivid dream that bubbled up some deep guttural sorrow. Grief tends to sneak up in those quiet, dark moments. I missed my mom so much, and the dream woke me with a heavy pit in my stomach. I didn't want to keep Mike up, so I crept downstairs to the spare room, got tucked under the covers, and just laid there.

    Hot tears flowed from my eyes. Very few thoughts ran through my head, just a longing and a deep misery at the reality of never hugging my mom again. I would never sit across from her in the living room while we talked about everything under the sun for hours. I would never hear her voice again or her contagious giggle. She would never see her granddaughter grow up. *Oh my God. I still needed her.* This was when the panic would set in.

She would never see her granddaughter go to school, drive a car, wear a grad dress, or become a mother. I had so many questions for her about motherhood. I was married with a child, but I had never needed my mom so much in my life. That would be a common theme in the coming years. I wanted her in the early days when life was robust and good, but I would need her, even more a decade later when things began to unravel.

As I laid in the spare bed, I allowed the deep grief to surface and then I began talking to my mom. It was strange because it was almost as if I could hear her talking back, not in an audible voice, but as part of a deeper connection. This was one of the many intuitive moments that showed themselves in my life. Now that I was open to them, they began appearing more and more. I went into a deep meditation, my mind went blank, and darkness came, just like I asked for. I was in deep pain and didn't know how else to make it stop. Sleep felt like the perfect cure.

When I woke, it was officially Mother's Day, and I knew Mike would have a special day planned. But first, I needed to lie in bed and process what had happened. Tears started falling again. But this time, they were tears of gratitude. I laid there in awe, processing it all. My mom had come to me in the most vivid dream I have ever had. This dream was a Mother's Day gift from her to me.

My mom was a beautiful woman, but in this dream, she was stunning. She was wearing a sparkling blue ballgown - Cinderella style. She had the most adorable smile, and she was twirling, and everything was blue. Blue dress, blue sparkles, blue aura. As Mom looked at me with the most intense feeling of love, she spoke these words as clear as day.

"Happy Mother's Day, Sheri . . . and Congratulations, you're having a baby boy."

And with that, she twirled out as mystically as she had appeared.

I laid there stunned. I touched my belly. I went upstairs and crawled into bed with Mike. I curled up next to him and started cuddling him. He rolled over and put me in my favourite spot, tucked inside his arms, and he kissed my head and wished me a Happy Mother's Day.

"Mike," I whispered.

"Hmmm?" he whispered back.

"I think I'm pregnant." A tear rolled onto his arm. He squeezed me closer.

"Oh, babe," he replied. "It will happen when it's supposed to. You think too much." He ran his palm over my head and down my face, a gentle reminder that my Gemini brain needed a time out. Something he was used to doing as my fleeting thoughts raced in multiple directions at any given time.

"This is different. Mom came to me and gave me a message." I paused, not sure what his reaction would be.

"It was so clear, Mike." I was sitting up at this

point, energized by the feeling of having Mom so close. "Mom came to me and told me we're having a baby boy. She actually said *'Happy Mother's Day, sweetheart.'* Like this was her gift to me. Everything was blue and sparkly, and I just *know* I'm pregnant, and we're having a boy!' I rambled on, talking fast.

Now I was wide awake, sitting up, and saying those words out loud made me bolt out of bed. I told Mike I would have a workout, shower, and run to the store, so he and our little girl had time to "surprise" me. Although I bought a pregnancy test that day, I didn't take it. A tiny part of me was skeptical and worried about being disappointed. I wanted that dream to be true. I really wanted to relish this magical gift from my mom. To my delight, within days, my pregnancy test confirmed what I had been hoping for.

This pregnancy was not so easy. I was constantly nauseous and therefore grateful I was a stay-at-home mom because I felt awful. I couldn't keep food down for the first four months. I remember being in the grocery store and feeling waves of nausea come over me. Our toddler was sitting in the grocery cart, babbling away. But even the thought of concentrating on what she was saying was making my head spin. And then it hit me. Leaving my grocery cart in the middle of the aisle, I grabbed her and ran in the direction of the car. I projectile vomited in the parking lot. I thought I was inconspicuous behind the vehicle, but I'm sure I wasn't.

My little girl stood beside me, wide-eyed and concerned.

She patted me, consoling me, "Mommy, it's okay, Mommy. You have a sore tummy?" She asked in the most comforting way only a two-year-old knows how to do.

I looked at her with wet eyes and said, "We have to go home, baby. Mommy needs to lie down.'

We drove home and laid down watching Dora the Explorer. I was a happy soul. I knew these intense symptoms meant that my baby was thriving and growing. Lessons I learned from the baby that I lost.

The pregnancy flew by, and I began feeling more like myself by my second trimester. By now, we found out we were having a boy. The ultrasound confirmed what we already knew.

Time began to fly by, and all of a sudden we were planning for Christmas. But really, we were preparing for a snuggly little bundle swaddled in blue; Christmas just happened to be around the same time. My due date kept changing, but it didn't matter; I knew I would have a baby by Christmas.

Looking back, this pregnancy was a nice distraction because it was my first Christmas without my mom. I missed her a lot during that pregnancy. I was so thankful to have Mike's mom, and I think my loss made us closer. I appreciated Grace so much now. She always wanted to know how I was feeling, and I came to rely on her weekly phone calls. Our relationship became more like mother and daughter. I was so grateful that our children had one amazing grandma left to dote on them.

Two weeks before Christmas, the contractions came. I was so happy, secretly hoping to have him before Christmas. We called some family who came over to look after our daughter, and then we went to the hospital. Once admitted, the doctors weren't sure if they should keep me or send me home.

The contractions were mild, and things were progressing at a snail's pace. Thankfully things began picking up, which justified not sending me home. I was able to get my pain meds this time around. But something didn't feel right - another gut feeling I had. Things were happening much slower this time.

Our son was born in the wee hours, and immediately I knew something wasn't right. The nurses whisked him away to the other side of the room. I saw how they looked at each other and locked eye contact. Their eyes were trying to conceal their growing panic. *What was happening? Why was my baby on the other side of the room and not with me?* Something felt off. Then it hit me.

He wasn't crying.

Mike and I looked at each other, and his face said everything. He was trying to calm me and reminded me that the medical team would figure out what our baby needed. But they were telling us so little as they tended to him on the other side of the room. I was becoming hysterical at this point, and suddenly the room felt like it was closing in.

Cry. Baby, please cry!! I kept praying. The nurses were trying different things, flicking his feet, unswaddling him, and putting him on my chest. They had paged doctors who were taking longer to come than they liked. Their concerned eyes kept darting to each other, and we picked up on what no one was saying. Time was running out. They wrapped him up and put him on my chest. I snuggled him and pleaded for him to cry. He made these tiny grunting sounds, and I begged him to breathe.

I don't remember anything after that. But I know I fell asleep, and Mike went home.

As I sit writing this, I want to call Mike to ask him how this part of the story goes. Why and how did I fall asleep, and when did he go home? That's when grief hits like a paralyzing tidal wave. There are pieces of this story that I will never know. I have no one to share this memory with. No one to fill in the gaps. This reminds me that I lost more than a husband through his death; I lost the shared part of our brain.

When I woke up, everyone was gone. I paged the nurse and asked to be taken to feed my baby. I thought he must be hungry. I had slept for over three hours. The nurse told me she would bring someone to take me to see him. I remember being confused, groggy, and feeling a lot of anxiety. The nurse arrived, and we went to the third floor. When the metal elevator doors to the unit opened, I was stunned and speechless. I realized I was in the neonatal ward surrounded by tiny babies and their life-sustaining machines. I immediately panicked and asked where my husband was. The neonatal nurses didn't know and were surprised that I hadn't been filled in about our son. *Filled in about what?? What is happening?*

A doctor pulled me aside, showed me some X-rays and explained that his tiny lungs weren't fully developed. They assured me it could be common for boys born a week before term. *Where is my baby??!!* I was panicking inside but needed a calm brain to take all this information in. I just wanted to hold our son.

When I was taken to my boy, I was stunned speechless. He was in an incubator full of tubes, naked, with a diaper on. I went to him and didn't know what to do but touch his little hand through the tiny window. My tears fell, and my anxiety skyrocketed, but I was assured he was now stable. They had to put him in a deep sleep because he was feisty and kept ripping his tubes out. Deep sleep . . . I think the word they used was *coma*, but again I don't have Mike to confirm these details.

I wasn't able to feed my baby for days. I had to pump milk, and he was fed through a bottle when he was strong enough. Until then, he had a feeding tube.

I made my way back to my hospital room and called Mike. I was hysterical and livid that he wasn't there. I think he had been sent home by the nurse to get some sleep. *Again, details.* He was walking out the door when I called and was by my side within minutes. I felt better when he showed up. His calm, deep voice made everything feel like it was under control.

Mike looked so helpless seeing his son for the first time. I remember him holding my hand, telling me everything was going to be okay. Over the next few days, he went back and forth to be a parent to our little princess waiting at home. But she was confused about everything, and one day she took scissors to her hair and cut it all off. From then on, Mike stayed home with her, and I stayed with the baby. The two of them made the most adorable sign for his incubator, complete with her handprints. She really wanted her brother to come home. Over the course of a couple of weeks, our baby boy became stronger, and I was able to hold him and feed him.

Our son was discharged from the hospital just in time to have Christmas at home with our new little bundle. We spent a lot of time with family and friends and made beautiful holiday memories. We were exhausted by the end of the festivities, but our family felt whole, and the house felt complete with our new addition.

But two weeks after Christmas, I could tell something wasn't right. The baby had a cold, and something was off. After going to two walk-in clinics and being sent home both times, I just knew in my gut that something was wrong. I trusted my instincts, and I became insistent. Finally, I took him to a third doctor, who told me to get him to the hospital immediately. He said our baby couldn't breathe, and we didn't have much time. He offered to call an ambulance but said if I left right now, I would have time to make the drive. He instantly called the hospital and assured me they would be waiting for us. I hysterically called Mike, and he left his shift to meet me there.

Arriving at the hospital, our baby was again whisked away by a waiting medical team. The X-rays showed he had pneumonia. On his fragile lungs, this was not good news. He was admitted, and again I found myself by his side while Mike bounced back and forth between home and hospital. Our son was given various rounds of antibiotics, but nothing was working.

My memory of this time is foggy at best, but I distinctly remember speaking to the pediatrician wanting an update. He informed me that they had tried two different types of antibiotics and had one more to try. He was concerned about how resistant this strain of pneumonia was, and because our son's lungs were already compromised when he was born, there was a possibility that he wouldn't be strong enough to pull through. We were told to prepare for anything.

Everything stopped when I heard those words.

A calm came over me as the impact of his words sank in, even though my body wanted to panic. I finished my conversation with the doctor. Then I slowly walked down the hall to my son nestled in his hospital crib and had a candid talk with him as if he were a teenager who needed guidance. Quietly and softly, I told him I was giving him every ounce of energy I had in me. I told him that he was going to be okay and that I needed him to do his part, and the doctors would do theirs. At this point, all we could do was wait and see how he responded to this last round of medication.

To our relief, after a couple weeks in the hospital, the last round of antibiotics worked, and we were able to bring our son home. I watched him like a hawk from that point on. Overprotective doesn't begin to describe it. By now, my intuition was in full swing, and I was less skeptical of the intuitive events that started to take place more frequently. I learned to trust them. Like little gifts from my mom.

Thankfully, that was the end of our son's health scare. We brought home an incredibly happy baby who was always full of smiles. He loved to cuddle with his dad, and they would often be found having a nap together on the sofa while watching a football game. Mike was excited to teach his son about the things he loved. He couldn't wait to buy him his own snowmobile and teach him how to skate and throw a football. Our family now felt complete.

I have always been fiercely protective of this boy; there's a part of me that has always felt guilt for how he came into the world. So, I've made a point of making up for it over the years by smothering him with hugs and kisses. *Annoying* is the term he would now use to describe me. He will understand and learn to appreciate it one day.

CHAPTER 13
WE WERE BLESSED

After our little boy was home and healthy, we settled in and I began to adjust to life without Mom. Mike and I continued to build our suburban life. We were close with our siblings, always getting together with my family, driving to his sister's farm, an hour away, or driving down to Regina to spend time with his parents.

Mike began working in a newly created unit within the RCMP. It was a drug and organized crime enforcement team that was integrated with the Saskatoon Police Unit. He excelled there and loved the challenges and flexible hours. He got so much satisfaction doing lengthy investigations instead of the highway patrol he had been used to.

But parts of his new job were complex because he

could rarely talk about his work. It was all top secret. Often, he was the unnamed lead investigator on many headlines that made the front page of the newspapers. I was so proud of him, as I knew how much effort, planning, and patience went into each investigation. As the kids got older, they didn't believe their dad was a police officer because they never saw him in a uniform. He loved pulling out his old uniforms and surprising them - they were always awe-struck and fascinated.

We were preparing ourselves for some big moves within Mike's career. It was often suggested that he had what it would take to climb the ranks. He often saw himself as an Inspector, even if that meant moving to Ottawa. I was his biggest supporter and would have happily followed him around the country.

I could never understand how he could sit in the backseat of a vehicle, camouflaged under a blanket and do surveillance for hours. But he loved it. He loved the high intensity of organizing covert operations and the meticulous attention they required. It was his job to utilize various undercover techniques, as he kept the unit and undercover teams safe. He was phenomenal at what he did. Their operations would last for months, and it was nice to see him unwind and relax when they were over.

Sometimes we wouldn't see him for days. When it was over, he would take a break and then do it all over again. He had multiple phones, one for personal and a few for work. He had to establish relationships with criminals who divulged information about investigations, and they called him often. He was incredibly protective of the kids and me, and never wore his wedding ring to work so that no one could tell anything about his personal life. One time an informant called him and described me in detail. He had seen us out driving on the weekend. Mike lost his shit on him, and the experience made him a little paranoid after that. When we were out as a family, I knew he was keeping a watchful eye on everyone and everything.

Mike was a chameleon. He often looked rugged and sexy. His work allowed him to wear regular street clothes and grow a beard, and sometimes he even grew his hair out, depending on what was needed. I remember picking him up at the airport after he'd spent a month in Vancouver, and my eyes almost popped out of my head when I saw him. Two incredibly intimidating men walked out of the terminal. They looked disheveled but with swag and confidence as their eyes darted around the airport, looking for their families. Mike could grow a full beard in five days, and he hadn't shaved or cut his hair in a month, and his clothes were ripped and tattered. His partner, wearing paint-stained clothes, had a full braided beard, and his dark hair cascaded down over his shoulders.

People were grabbing their children close as they walked past. I even saw one woman kick her purse under her chair. But all our daughter could see was her dad. She ran up to him, screeching his name while leaving a cascade of pink sparkles in her wake. He scooped up his girl, and tears started rolling down his cheeks. As we made our way up to Mike, I had our son in my arms. We got enveloped in our favourite big bear hug. Mike plastered my face with kisses. He had hated being away from us for that long. It was so good to have him home again.

Mike's job was so demanding and unpredictable at times, it would have been challenging if I had worked full time. I loved staying at home with the kids in those days. Now that we were in Saskatoon, I knew I would soon have the time to return to school.

The upper ranks always made it clear they were keeping Mike in his role for as long as possible. He was terrific at what he did, and after he passed away, a member of the upper ranks referred to him as the "Gretzky of his position." His contributions to his unit were priceless. He was becoming a shining star and proving invaluable to any file he touched. Therefore, it was a blessing that I loved the simplicity of being home with the kids.

The kids and I spent a lot of time at the spray park and going for walks. We always had coffee dates with other moms, and the kids loved going to the daycare at the gym. I loved my afternoon naps, and the kids would snuggle in with me. Sometimes they watched a show, and sometimes they fell asleep. There was always music playing in our home, and you could often find the kids and me dancing, baking, or making crafts. They loved it when Mike would grab me and spin me around. He was an incredibly affectionate man, and he never left the house without a goodbye kiss and telling the kids he loved them. We were his world. Our house was always filled with laughter back then. Sometimes I felt like I was living a dream, as this was precisely the kind of life I had always pictured for myself.

 I was a health nut and enjoyed cooking healthy meals. Mike would pack a massive cooler full of homemade sandwiches, leftovers, and fresh fruit and take it to work with him daily. He kept current on fitness by reading books and googling new workouts. He loved having bulked-up arms, and I usually teased him about filling them with tattoos, but he never did.

 He helped me with my workout routines, and we would go to the gym together on the weekends and stop at Booster Juice on the way home. Walking paths surrounded our neighbourhood, and it was on these paths that Mike taught the kids how to ride their bikes. As the kids got older, they got involved in baseball and skating. Saskatoon was where our daughter took dance lessons and figure skating, and our son learned his love for hockey.

 As a family, we were very active and spent a lot of time outside, either at sporting events or just at home. We enjoyed keeping our yard impeccable. I made sure it was full of bright flowers, and Mike ensured there wasn't a weed to be found. We spent a lot of time on the two-tier deck we designed and built. During a rainstorm tucked under a makeshift tarp, Mike could often be found sitting on that deck. He loved the rain. It became his bonding time with his daughter. I would be inside all warm and curled up with our son, and those two would be outside in a makeshift fort. It was so relaxing to watch them. Mike's ability to appreciate the small things in life kept us all grounded.

Mike and I spent all our spare time together. He rarely went out with the guys after work; if he did, he usually invited me. I would get so embarrassed when he introduced me as his "hot wife." I would scold him, but he still always made me feel like the most beautiful woman in the world. He became the standard for a thoughtful husband, but his friends didn't always appreciate it. They often told him to scale it back because he made them look bad. This just fuelled him even more.

Mike was full of life and was often the guy at the table who would crack everyone up. He loved to tease and gave all his nieces and nephews silly nicknames, which they loved. He was the fun uncle who acted like a big kid. He would play tag, chase the kids, and scoop them up. With his deep voice and laugh, it was hard not to just to sit back and take in all that joy. He constantly put a smile on everyone's face, especially mine.

We made time to get dressed up and go out without the kids, which was always fun for me. I always loved an excuse to wear heels. Mike didn't enjoy going out as much because he was always on guard. His eyes were constantly darting around the room, assessing who was there. Sometimes we would walk into a restaurant and then walk right out because one of the targets of his investigation was there. Another time, he saw a bad guy he had been after for a long time. He didn't want to lose him, so we had to sit at a specific table. Mike positioned himself to keep a watchful eye on the guy. His wedding ring immediately went into his pocket and told me to do the same with mine. He would spend a lot of time on his phone on these rare occasions, and I felt like I was in a James Bond film. I had to ask him when it was ok to go to the bathroom. I teased him that I could drop a napkin or create a distraction, but he just rolled his eyes. "Just sit here and look pretty, Sheri; that's your job right now."

His work could take over our lives and often, I didn't mind, but it could become annoying. Sometimes we would walk as a family in the mall or at the Forestry Farm, and Mike would disappear. Poof. Gone. I'd turn around, and he'd be nowhere to be found. Then he would reappear out of nowhere. The kids and I began to accept this as the norm and worked around it. It seemed he could never completely enjoy himself on his time off. He was always paranoid that someone would see the kids and I and use that information against him.

We were mostly homebodies. It was easier on us, and Mike could relax a bit. We had weekend movie nights, and Mike would convert the playroom into a massive fort with lights and get the kids settled in with their favourite movie, popcorn and fruit snacks. Our Rottweiler would tuck in between them, waiting for the popcorn to fall. Mike and me would snuggle in the family room with drinks and snacks. It was our favourite place to be on a Friday night.

We enjoyed hosting and entertaining at home. Our house was often full of friends and family. He took the time to search through recipes and marinades and would go out and buy the groceries while I prepared the house. We would get ready, pour a cocktail and wait for the company to arrive. I ensured the house was spotless, and I'd have candles lit all over. The kids loved to help. Once our company came, we would all gravitate to the cherrywood and slate bar that Mike designed and built in the basement.

The kids loved their playroom, which had double French doors, a large TV, video games, and one wall full of Lego and board games. The opposite wall contained Barbie's mansion. We had a trampoline in the backyard and a basketball hoop in the front. The park was two blocks away, so the kids and their friends were always busy, running in and out of the house.

These years were so simple and easy. Mike would come home from work, and we'd talk about our days while we waited for dinner. He'd tell me about the latest operation they were working on and all the workplace gossip. He truly loved his job and loved to be able to share stuff with me. During this time, he was excelling rapidly at his job.

We had remained close with many of our La Loche friends, who were also Mike's colleagues. I remember one summer weekend when Greg and Jen and their kids came and spent the weekend at our house. Mike and Greg put on war paint and challenged all the kids to an afternoon of air tag. They acted like snipers, and these poor kids had no chance. These grown men plotted, had secret hand signals, and showed no mercy. I think they had more fun than the kids. Jen and I took in the entertainment in our backyard with margaritas in our hands.

We also hosted many CFL game festivities. Watching the Riders was a big deal during those autumn weekends. The kids would get all decked out in their green and white. Our son loved watching football with his dad, and they talked about the players and the plays; to this day, he still has a deep love for this sport and remembers watching those games with his dad.

Looking back, I just assumed this was the way it would always be because it was the way it had always been. We had a beautiful life together, a healthy marriage, and were still madly in love. Mike glowed when he talked about the kids and me. Everything we did was centered on our family of four, and our home was filled with laughter and love. I can honestly say Mike and I rarely fought. We never went to bed mad, and we had this amazing ability to talk everything out. It seemed normal to me; because that was the kind of marriage and family life I grew up with. I knew we were incredibly blessed in so many ways.

During these years, Mike fell even more in love with snowmobiling and spent a lot of free time with my dad on northern snowmobile trips. They took some annual trips with Dad's buddies to a fly-in camp. Mike loved those trips! They were rugged and exciting, and the stories were terrifying. They stayed in trapper's cabins, and it was Mike's mission to convince me to do it once, but there was no way I could keep up with the men. I knew someone would end up rescuing me out of the slushy lakes that they bragged about conquering.

The land around Dad's cabin was Mike's second favourite place to ride. There were many trails, open fields, and lakes to rip around on. We would often invite friends and family and spend our days on the trails with coolers packed with everything needed to make a fire and cook food. We always ended the day at the cozy log and stone cabin, sitting around the large firepit in the backyard. Even -30 C didn't stop us. Mike would bundle us in blankets and invite us out when he had the fire alive and blazing. I would sit there with a glass of red wine while the orange flames heated my face and hands. One Christmas, Santa bought new snowmobiles for each of us, even the kids.

No matter the season, the cabin was our favourite getaway. In summer, we would walk to the beach, and the kids would play on the swing set. We would go fishing, boating, or paddleboarding and were planning on buying a new boat. In the fall, the ladybugs would be all over the rocks and trees, and the kids loved to compete with their dad to see how many they could find.

Mike loved to work with his hands, and he always looked forward to working in the shop that Dad had attached to the cabin. I think this was where he could shut his brain off. He could get lost in a project, which gave his analytical brain a break. He had every tool at his disposal and would find projects to create. He would often ask me to design something for him to build. He made me a wooden curio and a beautiful wood and slate table set that we had in our living room for years. He built shelves for the kids and even carved wild animals into a tree trunk. Mike was a phenomenal artist, a hidden talent not many knew about.

The times at the cabin were so relaxing. We would visit with the neighbours, or sometimes just chill out on our own. The kids loved playing upstairs in the loft with their Legos and puzzles. My dad made a log bed that folded up into the wall, which he called the Magic Bed, and the kids absolutely loved it.

During these years, I became very close with my mother-in-law and aunts and grandma. I cherished any mother figure I could find. My mom's little sister would call almost every day, and we talked for hours. Sometimes it was about parenting, and sometimes it was to gossip about family stuff. We exchanged recipes and workout routines. There was always something to catch up on.

At this time, my mom's older sister had gone into cancer remission. She had been diagnosed with breast cancer shortly after Mom died but had been able to treat it. I checked in with her, too, especially since cancer was a strong theme in my family.

I was still going for regular ultrasounds under the direction of my mom's doctor. I still worried that I had an increased risk because cancer had taken my mom at such a young age. My mom's older sister had had genetic testing done a few years prior, but the results were negative. So, we deduced that cancer just seemed to be bad luck in our family. I never really put much thought into this anymore, as our life was full and busy, and we focused on creating happy memories.

CHAPTER 14
<u>THE LOSS OF GRACE</u>

When our son was in preschool and our daughter was in grade two, I finally decided to return to university. I finished my Bachelor of Education in less than two years and began my internship in the fall of 2010. I was interning at a school just outside Saskatoon and was teaching grade five. It was a dream internship with a very supportive staff. My supervising teacher was my age, married with kids, and we hit it off. I was very nervous about getting up in front of a room full of kids, but she was so organized and supportive, and it ended up being an easy introduction to teaching. However, about a month into it, we got some awful news.

Mike's mom had been diagnosed with aggressive cancer. We had noticed she wasn't feeling well at Mike's brother's wedding that summer. It all happened so fast. It seemed that her time was so short as soon as she was diagnosed. She was still so sweet and loving as she sat in her hospital bed while her family doted on her. Her main concern was how awful she felt because she didn't buy her granddaughter a birthday present. That is a perfect example of her loving nature.

She always bought our daughter little porcelain dolls with her birthday number on them. It had become their birthday tradition. This year, she told me where to go, and I found one with the number seven on it. I wrapped it up and gave Grace the card to fill out. I remember Grace's eyes welled up with tears when she saw her granddaughter open it. This collection was so important to Grace, and now having that little doll collection stop at number seven brings everything into perspective.

My kids remember that hospital visit. My son remembers his grandma rubbing his back as he lay beside her on the hospital bed. It all felt so surreal. I couldn't believe we were in the process of losing Mike's mom.

Mike was not taking it well. On the surface, he seemed okay. But I knew him to the core, and I could see the pain behind his tough guy facade. He spent a lot of time at the hospital by her side, and I know he felt helpless, which hurt him the most, seeing someone, he loved with limited time and knowing there was nothing he could do.

Cancer was striking our family again, and I was devastated that the kids were losing another incredible grandma. She was a sweet, gentle soul who lived for her garden and her family. Mike's mom passed away in the fall of 2010. We had a beautiful, simple, sweet funeral for her, just like she would have wanted. Although my kids lost their grandmas very early on, it was important to me that they knew and understood the women that they were. We always talked actively about them and told many stories. We treasured any piece of our moms that we could.

With both moms gone, I became incredibly close to my two aunts and my grandma. We chatted all the time on the phone. I needed them. Sometimes it felt like all the death and loss brought Mike and me closer as a couple. We understood each other on a deeper level, as we had grieved a lot together. We seemed to understand how precious life was and didn't want to waste our time on petty things. So, we made sure to create a life we enjoyed, even though a lot of pain and grief had gotten us there.

CHAPTER 15
<u>REARRANGING MY GENETICS</u>

As time went on, I began teaching middle school full time. We enjoyed the extra money and soon began planning family vacations and focusing on the four of us. We took the kids to Disney World one year and Coeur d'Alene the next. The kids were in sports, which kept us busy running them around and cheering on the sidelines. Our house was always full of their friends, who all lived in the neighbourhood.

Mike would always be the jokester, making the kids laugh. He could often be found playing mini sticks with the boys or teasing the girls about boys. If he brought home a work vehicle, the kids could push the buttons to make sirens and lights fill our neighbourhood. Looking back, I see how happy we were. How settled and comfortable the kids were.

We had been in Saskatoon for about ten years,

and I had been teaching for four of those when we began to get the itch that maybe it was time for something different. The kids were getting older, and our house was starting to feel small. We thought about upgrading our home and building something bigger in a nearby neighbourhood. It would give us projects that we loved, and we could finally afford to add some of the luxuries we had always wanted.

The school year was coming to an end, and I was wrapping up my grade eight classroom. We were preparing for the big grad celebration when Mike came home with some news. We were being transferred to Regina! It was music to our ears. We had many friends in Regina, and Mike's family was still there. It would give us the change we wanted, and I was excited about buying a bigger home.

Around this time, my mom's baby sister called with some news. She had been diagnosed with breast cancer a few months prior, and she was very positive about it and was determined to beat it. She had just finished her reconstructive surgery when she called to update me. She had undergone the same genetic testing that her older sister had done, but her tests had come back positive. When she called, she said she thought it would be a good idea for me to have this same genetic testing. Ovarian cancer is often in the same family as breast cancer. She had a number for me to call.

We assumed the cancer in our family was due to

random bad luck, but this testing proved that cancer was passed down in our DNA. Mike and I talked extensively about this. I knew what a positive result meant - invasive preventative surgeries would be the only way to avoid developing cancer myself. The hysterectomy didn't bother me as much as the thought of removing my breast tissue. My aunt was terrific to talk to about this. She told me her experience wasn't too bad, and she sent me pictures of her beautiful, reconstructed breasts.

Mike and I went to the hospital for the first appointment, which was a consultation. I was so nervous. The medical team was very candid as they walked me through the procedures and explained that no decision needed to be made immediately. But after speaking with the medical team, I knew what I had to do. I took the blood test before we left that day.

I was in my mid-thirties, the same age my mom was diagnosed with cancer. I knew how hard it was to live without her, and I didn't want to inflict that on my kids. I felt I had a responsibility to reduce my odds, given the information I was learning. I just wanted to start this process and finish as soon as possible. Looking back, I was so naive.

The test results would take a few days, and I was on pins and needles the whole time. Mike was very supportive and didn't seem to care that the surgeries would change my body. We had a lot of real and raw discussions about what this meant. He was adamant that he didn't care if my breasts were different; he just didn't want to lose me. That gave me peace of mind that I didn't even know I was looking for.

Within days of taking the test, I received a phone call that my results were in, and we were asked to return to the hospital. Once we arrived, we sat down and were told what I already knew instinctively. My results were positive.

There it was in black and white. My genes were missing some number sequences, and those missing numbers meant that my risk for ovarian cancer was 50%, and for breast cancer, it was 85%. It wasn't a matter of if; it was a matter of when I would get cancer. No one in my family had beaten it, and I knew I was looking at my death sentence on that spreadsheet of missing numbers.

Mike put his head in his hands, walked out of the room, and leaned against the wall in the hallway. A familiar calm came over me as I asked the nurse to please explain to my husband that this was *not* a cancer diagnosis. This was good news. I was the first in my family to find out *before* cancer took hold. I could do something about it, and that felt empowering. But my heart was breaking for Mike. I knew first-hand the anxiety and dread that comes with this type of news. I had lived it for so long as my mother's daughter.

I know Mike was scared to lose me, and I remember the way he looked at me. His eyes were tormented with a mixture of love, fear, and desperation. The helplessness I could relate to. He asked what the next steps would be, held my hand, and told me that we would do this together. He was going to make sure I was okay, and he would take off whatever time from work to ensure that.

Lost in our thoughts, it was a quiet truck ride home. The news impacted each of us differently, and we had a lot to process. I called my aunt when I got home and filled her in. I told her that the doctors would be calling me for my first appointment, and my first surgery would probably be the hysterectomy.

I was torn about this surgery. Many thoughts went through my head. What if we lost a child? What if I changed my mind and wanted more kids in a few years? Mike and I had decided years ago that we were done having children, and we were looking forward to them growing up and the freedom and travel that came with that. But there was still sadness about removing parts of me that were currently healthy. But I also felt like I had a ticking time bomb inside of me. So, part of me was panicking to get the surgeries done as soon as possible.

Mike started to come to grips with everything, which was a massive weight off my shoulders. My codependency was in full swing at this time, unbeknownst to me. Mike kept reassuring me that we were done having kids, and my idea of having a spare child was morbid. Our plan of having five rambunctious kids ended years ago when we decided to stop at two. Mike wanted to focus on the good, and if it meant we would be able to move forward from this, and remain healthy, then that's all that mattered.

Life resumed as we waited for the next steps. I began researching like crazy - hormone replacement therapy, what menopause looked like in your 30s, mastectomies, and reconstruction. I stumbled upon a story in a magazine and began reading that Angelina Jolie had just had the same surgery I was scheduled for. She had lost her mom to ovarian cancer, too. That was my sign. She looked so beautiful and happy. This was the universe giving me a message to do this, and it truly was a blessing. I was obsessed with finding any information I could, but what I should have been googling were the names of the top Canadian surgeons. I had no idea how important that was going to be.

CHAPTER 16
LIFE BEGAN TO SHIFT

It was now time to focus on our move to Regina. Our official house-hunting trip was booked, and the RCMP gave us a week in a hotel. Our time was jam-packed with a realtor, and we had many houses to see that week. On the first day we were excited and eagerly went from house to house. It was a long day, but nothing jumped out at us. The next day, Mike wasn't feeling well, but he pushed through. Again, no luck finding a new home.

At one of the houses, he tripped on a step and activated an old work injury in his knee. He was having trouble walking and needed to rest his leg. He had recently had knee surgery, so it was sensitive. By the end of the week, he could barely leave the hotel room. He was irritated, so I met the realtor on my own.

On one of the final days, I walked into a beautiful home that I instantly fell in love with. It was a large cream-coloured two-story with black stonework on the front. It looked like a dollhouse with its front porch and warm and bright colours. It had dark cherry wood floors and beautiful white quartz countertops. It had my spa ensuite with a massive corner tub, and the yard and basement were unfinished, so Mike had his work cut out for him. It was on the golf course and just down the street from an outdoor rink. Mike got the kids excited about the area, which was full of young families like ours.

We purchased our new home on the last day of our house-hunting trip. We were both super excited as it was an upgrade from our bi-level, and it had all the things we were looking for. I was excited because it had a bonus room upstairs that would be perfect for family movie nights. Mike was excited because it had an unfinished basement with unlimited potential and a bare yard that would need his time and attention for the next couple of years. I couldn't wait to fill the porch with red flowers in the summer.

It was time for my first surgery. I was scheduled with my mom's surgeon for my hysterectomy. She was a middle-aged woman with short blonde hair and large intense blue eyes. She had sharp features and a no-nonsense, almost cold demeanor. But she carried herself with calm confidence earned from decades of experience.

Mike and I went in for the consultation, and it

turned out to be an emotional day in her office. It began with a walk down memory lane for both of us. She said she remembered the day she told my mom of her diagnosis. She could still picture my dad sitting beside my mom. She remembered the fear and desperation in their eyes as they learned of the tumours that had grown unexpectedly large. It was a surreal moment for me.

She told me that memory of my parents had always stayed with her. I remember thinking she was probably similar in age to my mom. Then it dawned on me that Mom was perhaps one of her first cancer patients, and being similar in age was probably why the experience had made such an impression. Both women would have been in their mid-thirties, the same age I was sitting in her office that day.

She teared up as she told me she felt like she was giving back to our family by performing this surgery on me. She said it was a blessing that I would be able to outlive my mom and reassured me that she thought I was doing the right thing. I was scared and nervous to go on hormone replacement therapy, as I'd be in full menopause. But again, she reassured me that we could play around with the estrogen doses to ensure I felt good.

The surgery was a success with no complications. I was relieved. Dr. E came to see me in recovery and told me there were no tumours, and they had no reason to think there was cancer, but they were going to send some tissue away just to make sure. A relief, but all I could think of was that *I was sterile* - no more babies. I was in my mid-thirties, and both our kids were in school, but it felt odd because some of my friends were just starting their families, and here I was in full-blown menopause. Mike was very much my rock. I was up and down a lot, and he was the stable one who kept me grounded.

During this time, a ton of RCMP paperwork needed to be completed regarding the move to Regina. The kids were starting grades three and six in a new school and were both excited and scared. I was starting as a substitute teacher and was dreading learning a new school system. Starting as a substitute teacher was frustrating after having a classroom for so many years. Mike was starting his new position and was excited as it was at Headquarters and full of many promotion possibilities. Our new home was a busy place, and everyone was a bundle of nerves. Depending on the day, we didn't know who needed the pep talk.

We were fairly settled in Regina when my next major surgery was scheduled. Mike seemed to be more tired than usual, but I just assumed it was the stress of the move, the new job, and everything else we had going on. I didn't discuss my breast surgery with him as he constantly seemed on edge. Something was different with him, but I couldn't pinpoint it.

I was downplaying my upcoming surgery, but I dreaded it. I hadn't even had the surgery, and it already made me feel ugly. I thought I would feel like less of a woman. I already felt that way after the hysterectomy, and that was a surgery no one could see. But removing my breasts was a whole different thing.

I kept thinking I wouldn't be a real woman if I needed hormones and implants to feel and look like one. I didn't want to feel like a plastic doll. My mind was always racing with what-ifs. I hated it. I would go to work with a smile plastered on my face and frantically google mastectomy scars on my break.

I would look at women and feel jealous that they didn't even know how lucky they were to be able to keep their own breasts. In the staff room, people would talk about normal everyday things, and I would zone out. I hated listening to topics that seemed so insignificant to me.

I began to feel like I didn't fit in anymore. I was lonely. I was scared. I didn't want to talk to Mike about it because I was nervous I would be voicing what he was secretly thinking. What if he was just as worried about the results as I was? I couldn't bear to hear that from him, so I acted fearless and confident.

But, on the inside, I was grieving the parts of me I was about to lose - by choice. I cried a lot about it in private. I started to have more baths, as my new stone tub was so soothing and a comforting place to shed some tears. Our move to Regina and fresh start were not what I thought they would be. We were both under a lot of stress, and suddenly my life was beginning to feel unrecognizable.

CHAPTER 17
NO TURNING BACK

The day I was dreading finally arrived. Mike and I drove two hours to Saskatoon for my surgery. I felt numb and like I was being led to the slaughter. I had plummeted into a self-diagnosed depression. I fully understood that I could not go on hormone replacement unless I agreed to remove my breasts, as hormone replacement therapy would increase my already incredibly high chances of breast cancer. There was no going back.

We arrived at the hospital, and I filled out the paperwork. I remember Mike's loving smile and warm hand on my shoulder, and he said I looked like a little girl in my blue, thin hospital gown. I was cold. The blue paper slippers did nothing for my frigid feet. Mike was able to sit with me when the surgeon came and talked about what she would do. My eyes filled with pools of tears that I refused to let fall. I had agreed to this already. I had to follow through. I knew I had to do this. But every fibre of my body wanted to run out of there.

I had a very long road ahead of me, and it was about to begin when I walked through those metal double doors into the operating theatre. Mike hugged and kissed me and told me he was proud of me and that everything would be fine. His soft, blue eyes locked with mine, giving me some comfort and peace, but my stomach felt heavy with remorse.

I hopped on the cold operating table and stared at the ceiling full of large shiny spotlights. I felt nothing. I refused all emotion. Feeling nothing felt better than my feelings of regret and self-hatred. I hated how happy the nurses were. I could see only their kind eyes above their blue surgical masks, but I resented them. They would go home to their everyday lives. They were about to transform my body, yet they would never see me again.

Finally, a doctor began to administer the anesthetic. I held her eyes with mine and softly told her it was okay if I didn't wake up. Her brown eyes widened slightly as she cocked her head to the side. Then I forced myself to chuckle softly, for her sake. To reassure her I was joking. But I didn't know if I was. I just wanted to sleep. I wanted to not wake up and deal with the months of recovery ahead of me. She put her warm hand on my arm, and I could see the sympathy in her eyes. She told me I was in good hands.

Then, like clockwork, she instructed me to count down from ten, and I drifted off into a blissful medicated slumber.

When I awoke, Mike was by my side. My weak hands immediately went to my chest. Thick tears welled in my eyes. I had these awful expanders where my soft breast tissue used to be. They were rock hard and grossly misshapen. They had jagged edges under my thin skin. *What the hell had I done?*

It was incredibly important to me that I keep as much of my natural body as possible. To my relief, the doctors were able to keep the tissue that I had requested. I remember reading Angelina Jolie having the same request. It's funny the details that can stick to a memory.

The nurses reminded me what I already knew: once my incisions healed, I would have to come back each week to get the expanders pumped up until my skin had stretched and could handle the implants. I felt like a shell of myself as I lay on that hospital bed. Mike was holding my hand, but I couldn't even look at him. I had never felt so frail and pathetic.

Mike had the truck all cozy with soft pillows and fuzzy blankets, and he treated me like a fragile doll as we began our journey home to Regina. As the days went on, I could tell something wasn't right. My incisions were very sore, and I couldn't move my arms, and then my incisions began to turn black. I was panicking. I tried to get hold of my surgeon, but I couldn't get through. Finally, her staff suggested I go to my family doctor. Mike took me in, and I was given an antibiotic to treat the infection. Mike was livid at the follow-up care I was receiving. He let my family doctor in Regina know, and they both agreed to keep a closer eye on me.

After a couple of days, it became apparent that my infection was not under control. The antibiotics weren't working. I spent a lot of time on the phone still trying to get through to my surgeon and a lot of time in my doctor's office, and now he, too, was trying to reach my surgeon.

He tried to get other surgeons in Regina to take me on, but none would, and I remember going through a period of intense anxiety. He even wrote a letter to the College of Physicians and Surgeons because my aftercare was so poor. He told me that, worst-case scenario, I could go to Emergency because a plastic surgeon would have to be assigned to me then. I was scared because these complications meant that the scars that were forming were four times the size they should have been. I had to get this infection under control.

I was trying to figure out how not to have my husband see me as a burden. He was working full time, taking care of the kids, running them to activities, and then had to take care of me and deal with my skyrocketing anxiety. I was ashamed of my surgeries and didn't want people to know, so I relied on Mike for everything.

Something was shifting with Mike, but I didn't know what it was. Subtle changes were happening. He seemed distant sometimes, and now he would snap at the kids and me more often. He had zero patience. Sometimes his behaviour really didn't make sense.

An example of this was when I asked him to go to the store to buy some bandages and supplies, but he flat out refused. *What?* He told me he wasn't going to go, and I could figure out another way to get what I needed. *What the fuck Mike?* I was so mad at him as I lay in bed. I had no way to drive myself, as I couldn't move my arms past a certain point. I had no range of motion. I was in pain with infections, and Mike was being completely unreasonable and cruel for some unknown reason. I pleaded with him that day, but he just stormed out of the room and left me there, speechless and in tears.

I remember escaping to my spa bathtub and crying. I missed my mom. She would have taken care of me. I was hiding my pain from the world. Yet I had kids who needed me because they were going through their own anxieties of being the new kids, adjusting to a new school, in a new city. How could I be so naïve as to think I could just have these surgeries and nothing would skip a beat? I was mad at myself. I was carrying a lot of guilt. I felt like a burden on everyone. But I knew I didn't have the luxury of waiting it out; it would have been a matter of time before my body turned on me. I had been fighting the clock.

During this time, I relied, as much as I could, on my aunt for emotional support. But at this point, her cancer had returned, and she was going through her own struggles. This just magnified everything for me. I couldn't burden her with my issues when she was fighting for her health. I started questioning the point of life and couldn't make sense of mine, as it was becoming less and less recognizable.

Later that winter, I was finally healthy enough to begin the weekly trek to Saskatoon to have the chest expanders adjusted. For one reason or another, I drove myself every week on that prairie highway. Mike always had intentions of taking me but usually cancelled because of work or not wanting to take any more time off. Sometimes he wasn't feeling well. The first time he cancelled on me, I called Zena. We had remained close since our La Loche days, and she now also lived in Regina. Her husband was posted at Depot, and at this time she owned her own financial company. She postponed all her clients that day to drive me to Saskatoon. That was the last time I ever did that. I felt too guilty and didn't want to put our problems on others like that.

While waiting for Zena to show up, Mike stood in the kitchen, grabbed me, and just held me with guilt-stricken tears in his eyes, and apologized for not being there for me. He felt awful. I could feel it in his familiar bear hug. He looked terrible; his eyes were bloodshot, he was shaky, and I could tell he had barely slept. Mike squeezed me so tight and just kept apologizing. He wouldn't let me go. Something was so different. He seemed like a shell of himself. If he wanted to be there for me, then why wasn't he?

The weekly trips to Saskatoon lasted for a couple of months. Finally, I was ready to have my implants put in. I couldn't wait. I felt so gross and disfigured with those hard expanders. My surgery was scheduled in Saskatoon. The surgery and implants were a success for a while anyway, but these firm tear-shaped implants ended up rotating. The top became bigger than the bottom. Now I had breasts that truly were deformed. I was so sick of this whole process and all the complications. I had to get creative with the clothes I wore. It was absolutely awful.

As the months progressed, I came to terms with my misshapen body. I had no choice. Christmas came and went; it was the first Christmas that Mike basically slept through all the festivities with the flu. He seemed to get the flu a lot. He wasn't sleeping properly. He was always tired, grumpy, and run down. I noticed he was losing weight and not hitting the gym as much. He often moved to the couch in the middle of the night.

When he was home, he could usually be found on the couch. I usually let him rest because he seemed to have nightmares, which started to intensify. They could be so violent. I would try to soothe him, and when he woke up, he was confused and often really angry. He usually downplayed it and never wanted to talk about it. I just assumed he needed a better bedtime routine. So, I would encourage him to read and take melatonin or come to bed earlier. I thought maybe it could be stress from his new position at work. He was saying so little, and all I could do was try to fill in the blanks.

He spent a lot of time finishing the garage and would often spend his evenings getting lost in his projects, but it was different now. Usually, he would take the time to teach the kids how to measure and how to use each of the tools. But I noticed he just wanted to spend more time alone. I started thinking maybe he just wanted to get the tasks done and didn't want the distraction of the kids.

It made me sad how much our life had changed in less than a year. We didn't have the active social life we used to. Our house used to be full of family, friends, and laughter. But not anymore. We weren't hosting parties or dinners, and I was disappointed we weren't planning more things.

My health was now stable, with more surgeries scheduled, but I had it all under control. Mike's moods became more unpredictable, and inviting people over felt risky, as I wasn't sure if he would snap at me, and I didn't want to deal with the embarrassment.

I began keeping the changes I was seeing in him to myself. I started suspecting something much bigger was going on that I didn't know about. I began to assume things like alcohol, depression, or maybe even another woman were to blame for his behavioural changes. Then, at other times, I thought this could just be a typical slump after ten years of married life. My mind would wander all over the place, trying to figure out what was happening to our marriage.

As Mike became more irritable, I began distancing myself from him. I was exasperated that he never wanted to do anything with us anymore. When we were around each other, we began fighting more and more. He was rude to me and short with the kids. I would cook dinner, and he would refuse to eat it, or sleep through and miss it altogether.

Planning things to do as a family was difficult, as he wouldn't commit. I created a family schedule to manage the kids' activities, but he wouldn't show up. I began making excuses to hockey coaches and other parents. It became embarrassing when coaches would text me saying he wasn't showing up to help on the bench. I always lied and said he was tied up at work and unable to contact them.

His secret drinking was confirmed when I found an empty bottle in the garage. His denial started yet another fight. I began to think I was going crazy, and Mike was quick to assure me that I was.

CHAPTER 18
KARYS LAYNE CANDLES

Our house had become increasingly chaotic and unpredictable by our second year in Regina. Mike hadn't been diagnosed with PTSD yet, but our family was really suffering. It was a very confusing time before Mike was officially diagnosed. It was obvious there was a problem, but neither of us could pinpoint what it was.

    I had now come to terms with my body and had accepted the changes that had taken place. I was busy focusing on my new grade eight classroom. At home, I picked up the slack and got used to thinking on my feet, acting as both mom and dad on any given day. There were usually signs and clues as to which way things were leaning, but I was getting tired of second-guessing myself.

    My beautiful spa tub was my sanctuary. I was becoming really unhappy and didn't know what to do about it. I savoured that quiet serene time in the tub. That was where the world stopped for a few hours as I surrounded myself with candles and bubbles.

This was when I decided to teach myself how to make candles. It was a distraction and a way to kill time at home. I would get lost on the Internet researching tutorials and recipes. I started ordering sample sizes of wax and wicks and different oils. I was excited when the packages came, giving me something to focus on.

I was terrified the first time I melted the wax on the stove. I thought I was going to blow up the house. But it wasn't that bad. It was similar to baking. I melted my first measurement of wax, waited for the right temperature, and then added the oil. I waited a few days before I lit the candle; to my dismay, it was a complete flop.

This began my love affair with candle-making; getting the recipes and containers just right. Whenever I changed a container, I had to change the wicks and the recipe. It became incredibly detailed, and I had to start documenting my every move to track what was working and what wasn't.

I learned which companies offered the best oils, and I began to get picky about the type of wax that I used. I liked the soy wax because it was softer, and I found something about the creamy burn pool soothing.

Mike and the kids began to look forward to my testing days. The house always smelled amazing. I started to feel guilty about spending money on this hobby, but

Mike always assured me it was fine. He always supported things I wanted to do, even when I was using it as an escape from his confusing and unpredictable behaviour.

Soon after, I discovered wooden wicks. This changed everything. I had to change my wax and oils, noticing their burn was much more finicky. But that's what I loved about them. The fact that you had to tend to them like little bonfires. They needed constant attention, and I could get mesmerized by the glow and the faint little crackling sound they made. I was in love.

I ordered more oils, and things were getting exciting. I had narrowed down my supply chain and started understanding what worked and what didn't. I couldn't wait to come home from work and make or test my candles. It was my little escape. I started not to notice so much on the days when Mike was checked out.

My artwork started similarly - first by accident and then with a passionate fury. My dad had a company in Saskatoon and a painting on his office wall that he hated. But it was on a beautiful large canvas. One day, when I was in his office, he asked me what he should do with it. He wanted to throw it out. But I had an idea. I asked him if I could take it home and paint over it. My creative bug had been ignited.

I took this painting back to Regina with me and set up a makeshift art studio in the basement. I bought some paints and began to think about what I would create. I had no idea if I was any good or what I was doing, but it seemed like a fun challenge.

I painted over the canvas with white, giving me a fresh slate to work with. I chose a forest scene I thought my dad would like, and I got to work. I painted that scene in a matter of days. I got lost in it.

I couldn't wait to come home and paint after work. I loved how I could just disappear downstairs. Sometimes my son would shoot hockey pucks on his net in the basement, and my daughter would set up a little painting station beside me. But most of the time, the space was mine alone.

I presented the painting to my dad for Father's Day, and he loved it. It was the first of many more paintings to come. That was the accidental part of my artwork; the passionate fury came shortly after.

One day, I was furious with Mike after one of his outbursts. I disappeared into the basement after we got into a huge fight once again. I needed to collect my thoughts. He could be so mean and say such harsh things; I never knew what sparked it.

My head was spinning, and I started pacing, and then I saw my makeshift art studio. I stomped over to it and threw up one of the canvases leaning on the wall. I tossed silver metallic paint on it and didn't care where it landed. I was in a personal storm, and now I was creating one with paint.

I added black and white paint and then flakes of glittering gold. I kept adding to it, not even realizing what

I was doing. I needed to exhaust myself and unleash the fury in my body. I finally walked away and slid down the wall in the corner. I couldn't even look at my painting; I didn't care what it looked like. I didn't paint it to be seen. It was an outlet for my anger and my hurt. And it worked.

The next day, I went downstairs to see what I had created. It wasn't as horrible as I had imagined, but I had no idea what to do with it. I set it against the wall and forgot about it. A few weeks later, I went to an art supply store and purchased different hues of paints in various mediums. I wanted to be prepared for the next time I needed an escape.

I spent a lot of time throwing paint on canvas. Eventually, Mike started buying me large boards, and then he fell in love with some of the paintings and even made frames for them.

Our relationship is hard to explain because it felt as if I was married to two different men. There was the man I fell in love with, who adored me, but sometimes he would revert to someone that the kids and I couldn't be around. It sounds odd that he would support the same hobby that his toxic behavior pushed me into, but he always, eventually, acknowledged his outbursts and held himself accountable. I think he was scared by the way his behaviour affected us.

As time went on, we muddled through with our coping mechanisms. Our house became full of my paintings, which says a lot about the state of our marriage. We had a lot of wall space, so I began hanging them. But I really didn't like them. They reminded me of the state of mind they were created in.

One of our neighbours was mesmerized by one of the paintings that hung in the front entrance. She asked where I got it and was shocked when I revealed that I had created it. She wanted to buy it, but I knew the energy it carried, and I didn't want to give that away. As time went on, she would ask if I had changed my mind every time she came over.

A year after Mike's death, I just couldn't look at that painting anymore. It made me sad - it teleported me to another time and place. It was my first painting, and it had been created with a lot of confusion and pain.

One day, I decided I didn't want it hanging on my wall for one minute longer. I had other paintings that caused me less stress when I looked at them. I called my neighbour and said I was finally ready to sell it if she still wanted it. She was elated. An hour later, she sent her husband over with the money.

The painting was gone, and the energy was removed from my walls. It was almost magical how the energy changed in someone else's hands. It still hangs in their house today and looks beautiful in their living room. It still makes me pause when I see it again, and I can't help but get lost in it. I see something different than everyone else. That was the first time I realized energy could be transformed - something negative could be converted into something creative and beautiful.

Our family had become different. Sometimes we were like our old selves planning weekend getaways and dealing with parenting issues as they arose, yet we shifted to adapt to a new chaotic way of living. I had no idea what our life would be like long term. I was more guarded now because I couldn't trust Mike's erratic behaviour.

By now, I was confident in my candle recipes and had begun designing a brand. I wanted to name it after our mothers, but I wanted to be creative with the names. Eventually, I just had to make a decision, and Karys Layne Candles was born.

Karys is Greek for Grace. That was Mike's mom's name. His family is not of Greek heritage, but I fell in love with the name when I found it. Layne is a play on my mom's name, Elaine.

I came up with a perfect font and found a graphic designer in Calgary who converted my font into a format I could use. Then I created the honeycomb design. I'm not sure why this was important to me. But bless this designer's heart because he had so much patience with my need for perfection. I chose silver and gold, as my mom loved combining white gold with yellow gold. So that is my homage to her. My mom loved her jewellery, so I wanted the candles to feel elegant and jewel-like. Mom was fancy like that. I found a supplier for the boxes and was proud at what I had created.

I learned how to build a website and buy a

domain name. Google was my savior. I loved working on these details in the evenings. It gave me a sense of purpose. Then I had an idea while I was out for lunch with Zena. I wanted to do a photoshoot with these candles, but I didn't want anyone to know it was me. I booked a photographer in Saskatoon who assured me she could bring my vision to life.

I arrived at the photo shoot with baskets of props and a ton of candles. It was such a fun and creative day. My body was still disfigured at the time, and my breasts were upside down. When I told my photographer my whole story, she had tears in her eyes. She told me how beautiful I was and that she wanted to capture my feminine side. What she created stunned me. She captured a beautiful blonde woman who was sensual and sexual. I used to always feel like that, but I hadn't felt that way in years. Seeing the photos ignited something in me, and I realized I was more than my deformed body. I was still a beautiful woman. She had captured that, and I will be forever grateful because this was one of the turning points in my life.

It took me a year to create the website, and then I started a blog about resiliency and finding my fire. My inspiration came from my surgeries and overcoming the challenges that my family could not. I wasn't ready to tell the world who I was, but I knew I had turned a corner in my understanding of what my body had been through. I felt stronger. I felt empowered. I felt feminine. This was the best side hobby I could have stumbled upon. It was healing me. It took me out of the hellish reality our home had become. As I was getting stronger, my husband seemed to be going downhill fast.

CHAPTER 19
THE CHAOS OF PTSD

Fights, silent treatments, and passive-aggressive behaviours became the norm in our home. Patterns were developing, and I didn't like them. The more fed up I got, the angrier Mike got, which led to arguments and anxiety. It was such an awful way for a family to live. Sometimes I think it would have been easier if we had fallen out of love with each other while we navigated these unchartered waters.

Instead, I was falling out of love with life. What was the point of being miserable all the time? I was worried that we weren't giving our kids the childhood they were used to and deserved. We used to be so happy, but nothing felt sacred anymore. Our home was a series of landmines.

I have a birthday I will never forget. It was the first week of June, and we planned a nice day at Wascana for our traditional family dinner. No matter what I tried, I couldn't wake Mike up in the morning. So, I let him sleep. As the day went on, I was hurt that he was ruining my day, but then I had a strong sense that I needed to keep a closer eye on him. I assumed he was passed out from booze. I tried to wake him. I was pushing on his arm, calling his name, yelling his name. I was tapping his face and moving his head back and forth. Nothing. Zero reaction. I went from anger to worry. I didn't want to leave the house; because this was the first time I had seen him like this.

Then he started throwing up everywhere. He couldn't even make it to the bathroom. I panicked as I ran and called 911. The ambulance arrived, and, by then, Mike was somewhat alert, but there was vomit everywhere. The two paramedics were young, and I remember them being very patient and kind to Mike.

They did their tests, had a conversation with him, and determined that he would be okay. Once Mike told them he was a police officer, I saw camaraderie and respect in their eyes. Miraculously, Mike was perfectly articulate when he said that I was overreacting. He convinced the medical team that he was fine - just having a rough day - and that his wife needed to chill out.

The paramedics pulled me aside and advised me to give my husband a break and to go easy on him since bad days happened. I stood there stone cold, taking in their patronizing words as if this was the first random shitty day he had ever had. I wasn't going to tell them that this was becoming a typical Saturday, and that today was my birthday. So, I kept my mouth shut, nodded, and swallowed tears. After they determined his most significant ailment was going to be an awful hangover, they left.

Mike was livid with me for calling 911, as I knew he would be. The rest of the day was absolutely awful. The neighbours started calling after seeing the ambulance, and I lied and said we had an allergy scare.

We would get back on track for a few weeks, and then another random conflict would arise. I remember being on my way out the door after a big fight. I was preparing to leave when I had to go back in the house because I forgot my purse in the mudroom. But the door was locked. Mike had immediately locked me out.

I knocked and knocked, but he ignored me. I could see him standing inside, and I was so embarrassed as I had no idea who was watching this show. I begged him for my purse through the door, explaining I just wanted my keys and phone. This went on for some time.

Eventually, he opened the door and started hitting me with my purse, and then pinned me over the railing and tried to flip me over. I have no idea what made him stop, but when he did, I ran as fast as I could to my car. The kids saw it all unfold while they waited in the backseat. That night the kids and I attempted to get a hotel room in Regina, as I didn't know where else to go. I had never felt so pathetic. Or alone. I was full of embarrassment and shame.

I always called Mike before returning home to assess what we'd be walking into. Usually, we would talk it out on the phone, and the kids and I would return home and find the husband and the father we missed so much. He would feel awful and would try to make it up to us.

Weekends were the worst due to the heavy drinking, and I hated what it was doing to the kids. No amount of yelling on my part had any effect. Once, he threw a gaming controller at me and missed. He threw it hard enough to put a hole in the wall two feet from where I had been standing. I was speechless. He rolled over and told me to leave him the fuck alone.

At times like this, I would often disappear into the basement and get lost in my metallic paints. It was my safe place, where I could go and clear my head, and for a brief pocket of time, I didn't have to live in my home. I began to hate myself, and I felt trapped. I didn't care anymore about anything.

Then one day, I was driving with the kids on Ring Road in Regina, and a massive rock flew off an overpass and hit the sunroof on my vehicle. Soft creaks sounded above, the telltale sound the glass was about to give out. I pulled over, grabbed the kids, and got them out of the car as the glass gave out and cascaded everywhere.

Shaken, I called Mike, who was at home on his day off. I finally got through. He was grumpy, but he showed up at the scene. Disheveled and mad, he parked behind my vehicle, sat in his truck and watched me. He wouldn't talk to me. Nothing. Then he told the kids to get in the truck. After they were buckled up, he peeled away, leaving me by the side of the road. I couldn't believe what I was seeing as my family drove away.

I have no idea how long I stood there before he turned around. When he pulled up the second time, he got out, threw his truck keys at me, and then got in my vehicle and drove it home, screeching the tires as he peeled away. I sat in his truck in pure disbelief. The kids were in the back, their faces wet with tears. It had been their pleas and tears that made him go back for me.

Eventually, a day came when he sat me down and apologized, saying he did not know what had gotten into him. He didn't have an explanation, only apologies and reminders of all the reasons he was in love with me.

Mike could be very emotional and candid, and at times like this, I would be reminded of the man I wanted to be with. He would sit the kids down, and we would have a family discussion about how his behaviour was wrong. He would tell the kids how much he loved all of us and that he didn't like it when he got so angry. He promised to try and fix things.

We would get back on track and have a nice BBQ supper and a movie night. It was these moments that kept me in my marriage. It reminded me of whom I had married but it was also very confusing. I didn't want to leave him because there were still too many good times, and I loved him more than anyone, and he always seemed so sorry. I also knew he was drinking more than I saw, but I could never find the evidence. It was becoming evident that his behaviour was fuelled by booze.

I began to engage less in the fights. But my silence fueled him even more if he was in a fighting mood. One time, I ignored his harsh words as he lay on the couch, being rude, and calling me names. When I disregarded him and started walking upstairs, he began spewing awful things about my mom. He knew exactly what he was doing. Filled with absolute rage, I ran over and, with all my might, I began punching him. I didn't even know I knew how to hit. He just sat there and took it. But it gave him ammo against me.

He laughed at me and told me he would have me charged. I grabbed his phone off the table, ran to the bedroom, and locked the door. I knew he could make one direct speed dial phone call, and I would be in trouble. He never followed me upstairs, and the silence was terrifying. I stayed in that room for a long time. I was shaking and crying. I had no idea what to do, or what he was doing. When I finally tiptoed downstairs, I peeked around the corner, and I saw he was icing his eye. It was red and swollen. I had given him a black eye.

He heard me and calmly asked me to come and sit down. He apologized and told me he deserved it and was impressed I could throw a punch. I asked him if I was going to be in trouble. He reassured me I wasn't. Unbelievable as it was, this conversation didn't even feel bizarre. He opened his arms, and I nestled against him as we sat in silence, heavy in thought. He kissed the top of my head, and I felt a sense of ease. I couldn't believe this was our life now.

He wasn't mad at me, but he was worried about telling people how he got his black eye. His buddy was supposed to stop by the next day to borrow a tool, and Mike didn't know what to tell him.

To my relief, he told the story that a hockey bag fell on him while he was bringing it down from the shelf. Our family was dysfunctional, and our home had become a place of constant chaos. Even as I share these stories, my heart breaks for how tormented he must have been. This wasn't who he was.

His nightmares continued to surface, but now with a vengeance. From what I witnessed, it was obvious to me that past traumatic policing events triggered Mike's nightmares. He seemed to be reliving past calls in his sleep. I had no idea he had seen so much death, and I felt helpless in the middle of the night because the intensity was out of my league. He was reliving car accidents, death scenes, and fight scenes. Often, all I could do was sit beside him and cry - I didn't know what else to do.

By now, I had started opening up to his family and

my dad about Mike's behaviour. Everyone was concerned about what was going on in our home. His sister would talk with me on the phone for hours, always checking in on us. She and my dad both texted the kids to ensure they knew they were surrounded by people who loved them. My dad confided that he was really worried about me. He wanted me to be in touch with him constantly because he was worried about how quickly things could escalate. I know what he was too scared to say; he was afraid that if Mike wanted to really hurt me, he could.

Mike would sit with my dad and reassure him that the kids and I were his world. He knew he needed to get help, and he would cry and tell my dad that the last thing he ever wanted to do was hurt us. Everyone was beginning to understand that Mike was battling some serious demons. He finally agreed to therapy, which made everything feel more manageable. The kids and I also started therapy. I was so incredibly thankful for our family's support during this time.

Again, things seemed to quickly return to normal; until Christmas rolled around. I made a beautiful brunch on Christmas morning, and the table was set with my gold charger plates. I had candles burning, and the tree was on display in the corner of the living room with the explosion of gifts waiting for the kids. The Grinch was playing on the TV, and the stockings were all stuffed and hanging from the fireplace. I was having coffee, waiting for the family to wake.

I wanted this to be a nice day for everyone, and I had put a lot of thought and effort into everything. After our traditional family brunch and gift opening, we were going to the farm to spend the night and continue with the festivities. We'd do a gift exchange and some snowmobiling with Mike's family. It was our annual holiday tradition.

The kids finally bounced down the stairs, all excited to see what Santa had brought. This was usually when Mike would get up. He and the kids would goof around and let them pile on top of him while the dog tried to get in on the fun. But this Christmas Mike refused to get out of bed, so I convinced the kids to watch TV for a bit.

Finally, I tried again to wake him. But he just rolled over and pulled the duvet over his head. I stood there, my eyes narrowed, as I watched him silently. I was done.

I decided I wasn't going to let him ruin Christmas this year. The kids and I sat at the dining table, and I told them Dad was making poor choices again, and maybe he would join us later, but if he chose not to, we would still have a wonderful day. I was done telling them he had the flu or worked late, or any other excuse. We ate the brunch I had prepared and waited until later in the day, when Mike finally rolled out of bed, to open gifts. He was a hungover mess and wasn't even apologetic this time.

Later that day, we got into a horrendous fight. He refused to come to the farm and just wanted to go back to bed. We were all packed up and late for his sister's meal. I was taking the kids to the farm, and he could do what he wanted. Mike threatened me if I left, he was going to lock me out of our house. At this point, I couldn't have cared less.

We yelled at each other, and he followed me around the house as I packed an extra bag and threw some clothes in for the kids. As this fight progressed, I was preparing for more than one night's stay. He threatened that I wouldn't have a home to return to if I took the kids. All I knew was that I needed to get the kids out of there. Everything about that house, and my marriage, was making me sick.

The kids and I finally got to the farm, and his family scooped us up and greeted us with hugs and love. They distracted the kids and made it fun with sled rides, giving them happy Christmas memories. They needed to be carefree kids laughing with their cousins and enjoying the festivities. They needed to be surrounded by love and to feel safe. The farm gave that to them, for which I am forever grateful.

At the farm, I knew I had to try and help Mike differently. I was feeling more desperate. I wanted to see if his friends had noticed a change in him. I knew I had to take our problems outside of our family. That was a big moment because there was no going back, and I was scared about what it would do to Mike's career and reputation. But it was time and long overdue.

I reached out to Greg and Jen. The RCMP had

recently transferred them to Regina, and I made the difficult decision to call them on Boxing Day. I was choosing to expose our secrets, and I didn't know what the backlash would be. There were many types of fallouts that could come from this decision.

With shaky hands, I made the call, but I still wasn't sure if I was going to tell them or not. Then, without warning, I completely broke down. I sobbed as I told them that Mike had slept through Christmas - and that we fought constantly. I told them I was at the farm and that I was pretty sure Mike had locked me out. I said I was scared to go home because I didn't know what was waiting for me.

They listened, never passing judgement. They kept saying this sounded nothing like Mike, that this wasn't him. They told me not to worry, that they would help, and reassured me that they were glad I called. They invited me over to talk.

I can't express in words what this moment meant to me. Telling our secrets out loud was incredibly scary and yet liberating at the same time. I felt less alone. I felt like I could breathe.

I left the kids at the farm and drove into the city. I was grateful they had invited me to visit with them, but I felt foolish waiting for them to answer the door. It was Christmas, and I thought I had no right to burden them with this. Jen answered in her Christmas pajamas and welcomed me with open arms. We sat in their living room, curled up with blankets and tea, and I began to confide about the walls of our home.

I explained I was worried about Mike and that I always lied to everyone, saying he was sick with the flu or making other excuses for him. I told them that he slept too much and I suspected he was drinking a lot, but I could never smell it on him, and he never drank in front of me. I couldn't find the evidence anywhere. It didn't help that Mike told me I was crazy all the time whenever I brought it up.

I told them of the rages and the names we called each other. I admitted that I developed a temper and didn't recognize who I was becoming. I cried too much and was always confused. I felt like I was micromanaging and trying to control everything all that time. I was exhausted. I told them that the kids saw and heard too much, but I didn't know what to do.

I talked about how he hated me sometimes, and then he would apologize and profess his love. He was always humble and kind and seemed genuinely scared because he didn't want to act this way.

They sat and listened with complete compassion and concern. They never judged or questioned one aspect of my story. Greg assured me he would talk to Mike and try and help him because he wouldn't let anything happen to his "Mikey Boy" as he called him. He called Morgan, a colleague/friend from La Loche, who was also recently posted at the Regina RCMP Headquarters, and together Greg and Morgan went to the house.

When they arrived, it was locked up like Alcatraz. Mike didn't answer the door. Peeking in the porch window, they could see Mike sleeping on the burgundy leather couch. He lifted his groggy head, looked over at them, and then laid back down. They relentlessly banged and knocked some more, and finally, to their relief, he got up and shuffled toward them. Mike went directly to the window and pulled down the blinds without even looking at them, completely shutting them out.

Wide-eyed and surprised, Morgan called and texted him, but he didn't answer. They had no choice but to use the key I had given them. Morgan and Greg couldn't find Mike when they let themselves in the house. They looked everywhere. Upstairs. Downstairs. He was nowhere to be found. They couldn't figure out where he had gone. They ended up finding him downstairs. He was hiding from them. It was like he knew he was in trouble and was trying to avoid it. They convinced him to come out, and they all sat in that basement and had a chat. He opened up to them that day, about lot of things.

Calling Greg and Jen was the best decision I ever made. It changed the direction of our life. Mike was able to open up to his two best friends that day in the basement. They all shared stories and understood each other's pain in a way that only fellow officers could. They broke down a barrier in my husband. He cracked and allowed the light in. This was the first step in the healing process.

Mike called me and asked me to come home. He was crying and apologetic and felt absolutely awful. I took advantage of having the kids at the farm so that we could spend some time genuinely getting to the bottom of this. Once again, I got swallowed up in his bear hug. I missed him so much. He seemed lighter after talking to the guys, and he was starting to understand that he wasn't alone or crazy; and reassured me that I wasn't either. He was beginning to realize that something had changed in him, and he felt relief that his friends could relate on some level. He wasn't mad that I had called them, and I think he was a bit relieved. He, too felt less alone.

Our life returned to a manageable state of normalcy for a while. We both felt better knowing we had more people to open up to. Finally, one day Mike told me candidly and in detail about the nightmares, which was no surprise as I had witnessed them countless times by this point. But then he explained the flashbacks, the smells, the screams, and how he couldn't get his head under control. I just sat and listened, and took it all in.

He had seen so much in his career, more than I ever knew. He had been surrounded by a lot of death and had feared for his life a few times. This was all new to me. It was a part of his job that he had wanted to shelter me from. He had attended calls where the women reminded him of me, and it scared him to think how quickly and close death could be. He had never told me any of this before. He said he wanted to protect me from it. Then he told me about the secret drinking. He turned to it to shut his brain off because nothing else worked. My husband was still in there and was now trying to find his way out of the wreckage.

His therapy became more intense, finally being able to begin dealing with those repressed traumas. He was officially diagnosed with an Operational Stress Injury called PTSD, and we started learning what that meant. I think we both felt a sense of relief that there was something we could put a label on and focus on. It made us feel like we had a little sense of control.

I continued to lie by his side when he woke in the night, terrified with nightmares. Sometimes he wanted to talk through what he was feeling. But I had to set some limits because some of the graphic details began to haunt me. I couldn't unhear it, and the visions in my head were very unsettling. They kept me up at night. I started to shed empathetic tears for people I had never seen or met, but somehow they were in my head. I couldn't imagine how it must have affected him, and my compassion for him increased as his honesty allowed me to see him on a deeper level.

I ensured he was eating healthy and going to the gym because all his doctors said that was important for his mental health. Meanwhile, he was anxious and terrified that he was ruining his career because of the stigma attached to mental health. His injury was now on file, and it embarrassed him. He was passed over for some promotions he had applied for, and now his ego was taking a big hit. This escalated his paranoia and anxiety. He was worried about people knowing the truth, even though he wanted to share his story - but he was too scared to open up. He didn't know what the backlash would look like. He was scared it made him look weak.

Things seemed to settle into a regular routine. We rarely allowed the kids to have playdates at our house because Mike and I were too raw and unpredictable. We were up and down. On track, then off. But at least we understood what the cause was, and we were learning how to navigate it all. It seemed to be part of the healing process.

The following summer, we planned a family vacation with our closest friends. We were excited to go to their family cabin, and the kids were at a fun age to go boating with. Since all the kids were similar in age, we knew we would build precious family memories again.

We loaded the black Dodge truck with food, water, toys, and a ton of fireworks, and it felt like a life we recognized. We drove up to the beautiful wood cabin with enough bedrooms for three families. We were all looking forward to a week of building new summer memories.

The first couple of days were great. The weather was beautiful, and we all lived on the lake. Jen, Kim, and I sat in our floaties and suntanned in our bikinis while the men entertained the kids. They went fishing, kayaking, golfing, and spent the later part of the day prepping dinner. We ate fantastic food, and every night ended around the blazing fire with many laughs. It was so lovely to be doing the usual activities we used to do. The kids were happy, and there was so much laughter filling the hot summer air.

But halfway through the week, Mike's behaviour shifted. He didn't partake in anything and kept going off on his own, only to return to be swallowed up by the couch. My stomach sank as the familiar feeling set in. He was not okay. He didn't want to talk; he just wanted to check out. I was panicking as my anger and frustration began to take hold.

Greg and Morgan noticed the alarming shift in Mike too. They searched high and low, looking for the bottle we all suspected he had guzzled, but no one could find anything. The biggest disappointment for the kids was when he slept through the thousands of dollars worth of fireworks we had bought. Greg and Morgan were putting on the light show, and Mike was passed out fifty feet away.

After the kids went to bed on the sixth night, I sat up with Greg and Morgan until the wee hours and talked. I didn't know what to do. I was so grateful that they knew what was happening, making it easier for me to open up. They were now very worried. This was not the guy they knew, and they were seeing it firsthand with their own eyes.

The following day the weather shifted, and it was cloudy and miserable, perfectly matching my mood. Greg and Morgan woke with a plan, and they coerced Mike to join them on the dock. They had three chairs waiting, and they all got comfortable. The three men sat there for hours and talked in the misty rain. That was another day that marked some significant changes moving forward.

I packed up the truck while they talked, and Mike didn't say a word as he prepared for the trek home. I drove, and he wouldn't even look at me on the three-hour drive. He was furious with me. He felt like we had all turned on him by holding him accountable. He was rude to me, and we fought the whole way home. I was fed up. I told him that I didn't want him back home if he was going to treat me this way.

I felt strong and was learning that if I didn't start demanding changes, nothing would change. I drove his truck to a family member's house and gave him an ultimatum: He wasn't allowed to come home until he agreed to go to rehab. I was officially done. We couldn't live like this anymore.

I contacted his family ahead of time and told them that we didn't have a good week and that Mike needed a place to stay. They were supportive and waiting for us.

When we arrived at their house, they had to

convince Mike to get out of the truck. He was refusing. There was a battle of egos, but eventually, Mike conceded, and I knew he was absolutely furious with me at this point. His piercing blue eyes glared at me, accusing me of pure betrayal, as I peeled away in the black truck.

CHAPTER 20
MIKE AND I SEEK HELP

Mike stayed away for three days, but it felt much longer. I didn't know what he was thinking or what would happen. I was scared it was the beginning of the end for us and that he wouldn't come home. Those blue eyes that used to hold so much love when he looked at me were unrecognizable the last time they locked mine.

To my relief, he finally called me to say he had made the difficult decision to go to rehab. Immediately, I got in the car and drove across the city to pick him up, and he gave me that big familiar bear hug. I was proud of him. Maybe we could get our family back on track after all. He came home and asked Morgan to call the Officer in Charge of Health Services to arrange the meeting. The next day, we were scheduled to meet with the doctor at RCMP Headquarters. Mike was both terrified and excited to begin this new chapter, and for the first time in a long time, he felt in control of his life again.

The following day, his two best friends picked Mike and me up. They had Tim Horton's coffees waiting in the car for us. Those men were incredible. They made the car ride light, and we managed to laugh a lot.

Greg is the silly one and can crack us up in a minute and even make light of the worst situations. Morgan is the sarcastic one, but he knows exactly what to do. He knows the people to call and really makes you feel taken care of.

The men were bantering and teasing each other, and Mike was even cracking his usual jokes about Greg's height. I smiled at the familiarity of it all. Once we arrived at HQ, there was a mountain of paperwork to complete, and the next thing we knew, Mike was scheduled to attend the treatment centre out west. His flight was scheduled for the next day. There was a lot to process in a very short time.

That evening we shared some precious and much-needed quality family time. We sat the kids down and explained to them that Dad was going to get help. We talked about what had gone on in our house. It was the first time we could really reassure them that things were going to get better. The kids were sad that Dad had to leave, but he promised them he would be back in time for our daughter's birthday that fall. He was going to do everything in his power to get better. There were many tears, and I remember feeling like *us* again. I knew this was the right decision.

I took Mike to the airport the next day, and he hugged me the tightest he had ever embraced me in his life. He was terrified. He didn't want to leave. I felt his intensity in my arms. He let me go. He kissed me, locked my face in his hands, and just stared into my eyes. He told me he was going to fix this. His promise was so intense and focused. Then he boarded the waiting plane and was gone for two months.

Nearing the end of summer, the kids and I had to prepare for the start of the school year. We hadn't had much time to process what had happened, but we decided to tell everybody that Mike was away on an undercover course in Vancouver. We weren't comfortable sharing the real reason with anyone, and it was no one's business.

Although we missed Mike every day, the kids and I were settling into a peaceful, predictable home knowing he was safe and getting help. Mike called every night at 6 pm, and it almost reminded me of his Depot days with the RCMP. He was on a strict schedule, and he loved that aspect of rehab. He was learning all about how his brain functioned differently and why. He was learning what PTSD was and how it can take a while to surface. His treatment started to put the pieces together to make sense of what he was going through. He learned about the altering effects alcohol has on the brain and neural pathways, and what this all meant as he began his new life of sobriety. He was so happy to talk to us every evening, and although he couldn't share details, I could tell he was making progress. He assured me that he had done the right thing and that things would be better when he returned.

When Mike returned home after his two-month stay, he was ready to conquer the world. He was healthy, fit, and excited about his new life, and the new beginning he had been offered.

I barely recognized him at the airport. He looked like a different man. He had so many muscles as working out became his new favourite hobby again. His eyes were a beautiful piercing blue and crystal clear. He was so handsome, and again he could take my breath away. He gave our family the bear hug that we had missed. He was happy and absolutely glowing. There were a lot of tears of gratitude as we stood together as a family in the Regina airport.

He started bringing me to the RCMP gym again, and it was our time away from the kids, where we could clear our minds in the weight room. He would put me on workout routines and help me with my form and technique - just like in the old days. I loved that we felt back on track. It reminded me of the days when we would go to the gym together in Saskatoon. He was energetic and enthusiastic and excited about life. He was grateful that we had stood by him.

We had some tough years, but I was relieved to have my husband back. He kept saying he had a bigger purpose, that he wanted to educate people, and he wanted to remove the stigma of asking for help and remove the fear of what it would do to one's career and reputation. He even talked about opening a coffee shop for police officers where it would be safe to connect and open up if they were having a bad day.

I will never forget the day he said to me, "Sheri, you have a problem too."

"Excuse me?" I recoiled when he told me that. It felt like a slap in the face. I instantly got defensive because I had been the one who ensured our family still functioned and to be told I was part of the problem felt insulting.

He was referring to my codependency. This was the first time I had ever even heard the word. He told me that he learned about how this coping mechanism was something spouses and family members often used to deal with the chaos of addiction.

I researched, but became repulsed at what I was reading. It was a mirror that revealed some deep childhood issues I didn't even know I had. It was hard to read that I was insecure. That I relied on others for my happiness. I put everybody else first and myself last. I struggled with my identity. I had no self-worth. I absorb other people's feelings. I am controlling and extremely critical - especially of myself. I didn't know how to set boundaries.

This was difficult to read and process. I was an amalgam of all of these things. I was textbook codependent. On paper, I thought I looked so pathetic. The more I read, the more I realized that I didn't really know who I was. I had given my power away, and my self-esteem was in other people's hands. It's why I had made excuses for Mike's behaviour and had turned a blind eye to what I suspected. I struggled to stand up to him because I was terrified of being rejected or abandoned.

As a true codependent, I made his behaviour about me, and that's why I spiraled so much. When he was rude, and mean, it made me hate myself because how he treated me determined if I loved or hated myself that day. I enabled shitty behaviour because I was so terrified of being rejected by him, so I would lower my standards. The more I read, the more I felt sick. But I wanted to know more. Mike and I went into Regina RCMP HQ, met with the doctors, and explained that I wanted to partake in the spouse program they offered.

The treatment centre included a week's stay for a member of the addict's family. I attended the program for one summer week and spent an unforgettable time with a dozen others. There were spouses, parents, grown children, and we all had the same issues - lack of self-love and fear of rejection. It made me more compassionate with myself to learn there was a reason I was the way I was. It was a relief to know I wasn't alone, and to be surrounded by people who were just as codependent as I was. I learned all about my behaviour and the fact that I put my self-worth in other people's hands based on how they treated me.

We are probably best known as people pleasers. I had become obsessed with trying to fix Mike, and I was doing it for different reasons than I thought. I learned how my panic for control caused its own special kind of chaos in the home and that it complemented his just perfectly. His chaos was loud and obvious. Mine was subtle and quiet.

It was humbling to learn that my reactions over the years had contributed to a lot of the drama and anxiety in the home. My role as caretaker crept up until I didn't even realize I had actually morphed into an enabler. I learned the importance of detachment and how to stay grounded when circumstances beyond my control were causing upheaval. I learned how to put my own needs first so that I could handle situations appropriately when I needed to. It was such an intense week and so educational. They had guest speakers come in, and we were able to learn all about the mind of an addict and what PTSD could do to the brain.

There is power in group therapy and finding people who *understand*. There is so much relief and healing in being surrounded by others who open a safe space to share shadow emotions and feelings. I was able to open up on a deeper level than I ever had in therapy and found so much comfort in being around others who were also going through the same thing. I was able to breathe again. I formed friendships that ran deep and still do. I, too, came home with crystal clear eyes and the tools for moving forward. I had a whole new insight and understanding of why we functioned the way we did. I learned about the hell PTSD was causing Mike and how I tried to make up for it.

When I came home, Mike and I had a lot of deep conversations, now that we spoke the same language. We could communicate candidly, and it felt like we were finally on the same page. That's when we talked about being a voice within the RCMP to help other families. We knew others were going through this and how hard it was to put your pride aside and admit you needed help.

I wrote a letter to the doctor at RCMP Headquarters offering my assistance to any spouse who needed support. Mike also met with them at HQ to say we were willing to help other families who found themselves in similar circumstances. We were called in and attended a meeting, and I remember feeling so grateful that we had been given this opportunity to give back. The thought of helping others seemed to give purpose to what Mike and I had gone through. Mike was doing great, and so was I. Things felt on track and, life was returning to a new, healthy normal

CHAPTER 21
THE DEATH OF MY AUNT

During this time, I was still very close with my aunt. We had our weekly phone conversations, and when I told her about the trouble I had had with my breast reconstruction, she told me my treatment had been completely unacceptable. She had had phenomenal treatment in Alberta and was really happy with her medical team. She explained my situation to her plastic surgeon in Calgary, and he agreed to take me on as his patient. It would be a few months until he could see me, but I could live with that. However, my aunt was not doing well. Her cancer treatments weren't working, and although she was incredibly optimistic, I was getting worried.

A few months later, I was standing at her gravesite on a gloomy day in February. I was in shock. Waves of grief and thoughts of my mom hit me like a tsunami. Memories of my childhood came flooding back to torment me, reminding me of all I had lost. Losing my aunt hit me as hard as losing my mom, and it was a reminder of the lethal gene that I was trying to outsmart.

 I couldn't leave that cemetery that cold winter day. I was frozen in time. I still remember the sound of snowflakes falling and snow crunching under boots. Mike held me, and all I could do was weep. I nestled my head into his neck and stood there limp as his arms engulfed me. I wept at how painful life could be. Mike held me for what felt like hours. No words were spoken. Our minds were racing, and we just let our thoughts fill the frosty air.

 When the funeral was over, we eventually made our way back to my aunt's house, where there was a beautiful celebration. Seeing my extended family and sharing so many laughs that night was comforting. The stories were flowing, and we could feel the presence of those we spoke about. My belly still glows thinking about how warm it felt to be surrounded by so much love.

 The following day, Mike and I drove our kids past our old apartments in Lethbridge, and we relived many nostalgic stories from our carefree college days. We lived about eight blocks from each other during our time in college. He showed them the street he used to drive down to pick their mom up for dates. He told them of the toilet paper/Band - Aid story, and we made fun of his sense of chivalry. He was so proud of that ridiculous story. Mike always teased me; that was one of his ways of showing his greatest affection. He explained to the kids that I snored too loud, and that's why he snuck out. I would slap his arm and roll my eyes. We had it down to a routine.

We were happy that day as we strolled down our memory lane of where our life began. The kids had a million questions about this city we met in. We circled past the bar where it all began, and we told the story of how neither of us wanted to meet each other that night.

We made our trek back to Regina the following day and settled back into life. Although these days of sobriety and normalcy were the new norm, they were short-lived. Mike began to slowly morph into the man he hated. But we were educated this time around. I knew what to watch for, and I wasn't so quick to rescue and enable. I made him more accountable while still trying to be understanding. But, to be honest, I was scared this was our new life, and I didn't know how long I could navigate these torrential waters.

Around this time, I had a consultation booked with my aunt's surgeon in Alberta, and I headed there alone. This was the second time I met with a doctor who had treated a family member who had passed away from this gene. The doctor was disappointed at what my complications and scars looked like and reassured me that he could fix them. I scheduled my surgery, and I was back in Alberta a few weeks later. By now, I felt like a pro going to these appointments on my own. I knew better than to put any more pressure or expectations on Mike.

This time when I laid on the operating table, I was excited. I felt I was going to get my body back. Thankfully, my surgery was successful, and I couldn't believe the results. My breasts were beautiful! The scars were the size of dental floss, and I couldn't believe the magical hands of this surgeon. I was one happy girl as I headed back home.

CHAPTER 22
<u>BOUNDARIES</u>

Our family was back in a good place, so we planned a family vacation to Maui for Easter. The kids were very excited. I was hoping a tropical reset would help us focus on new beginnings. I made all the travel plans, and we were going to take two weeks and stay at a fabulous resort. It had a gorgeous pool overlooking the ocean, and I had some relatives there that we were going to visit. I booked surfing lessons, catamarans, and a luau dinner, and we had plenty of time to hike, lounge, swim, and suntan. We were all super excited.

    Our daughter was anxious about flying, so Mike sat with her on the plane and was able to calm her like he could always do. Our adventurous son was busy taking in the views from his window seat. When we arrived, we rented a car and got groceries. The weather was beautiful, and we took in all the sights. We hiked through a bamboo forest and spent a lot of time on the beach.

On the fourth day, I noticed a change in Mike. He had slept in and was irritable when he woke up. He blamed it on the sun and said he thought he had heatstroke. By the fifth day, he refused to get up at all. I knew he was drinking and demanded he tell me where the alcohol was. I couldn't figure out how he even had time to go and get it. Then it hit me. He offered to run out for garlic bread a few nights before, as we forgot to buy some for our steak dinner. Everything clicked in that moment.

I looked everywhere for the bottle, but he was adamant that I was crazy. I ran out to the car and couldn't find it there. He yelled at me from the balcony, but I knew exactly what I was looking for. The bottle had to be somewhere. I knew it had to be in the car, and I felt like an intuitive force was guiding me. Then I found it—hidden with the spare tire. It was almost empty. I shook my head, and hot, familiar tears stung my eyes as I poured out the remainder. With a heavy heart, I knew what I had to do.

I went upstairs and grabbed the kids, my purse, and our passports. Mike sat on the couch with his head in his hands. He didn't say a word as I lashed fiery, angry words at him. I told him I didn't know if we'd be back. We couldn't spend the next seven days watching him drink himself into obliteration. He had recovery tools, and he needed to start fucking using them. I was beyond pissed. The kids and I went for a long walk on the beach. I couldn't believe he would do this to us on our vacation, especially when we were out of the country.

Hours later, we returned to the room, and I was prepared to pack and move the kids and me to another suite. When I arrived, Mike still had his head in his hands, but now there were tears on his face. He asked me to sit down and listen even though he understood if I chose to leave. He looked so sad as he explained that he had called his sponsor and would try and get back on track. We had a candid talk that night. He was trying. At the same time, I was trying hard to understand why it was such a struggle for him to stay sober. He felt terrible about everything when we went to bed. I didn't know if I was smart or stupid for staying. I kept thinking about the kids and honestly didn't know what was right for them anymore. The whole situation was wearing all of us down.

Somehow, we got our holiday back on track and put that day and night behind us. He never drank again on that trip. I knew because his relapses could not be hidden anymore.

We returned from our holiday and went about our regular routines. Teaching full-time kept me very busy, and Mike was busy with work. I started to be less anxious when Mike had off days and recognized it as part of his healing process. Ups and downs. Good days and bad days. The chaos wasn't as dramatic anymore, because I stopped reacting to it, and I no longer ran to our family and friends frantically asking for help. I learned to detach myself when I needed to. I had open conversations with the kids when Mike was feeling off, and I refused to make excuses. I wasn't protecting him anymore and held him accountable for his actions.

But then Mike started to have more and more bad days. I began to develop even tougher love for him and set firmer boundaries. He needed to spend more time away from home, as I didn't want him around us when he was unpredictable. The kids and I deserved to live in a peaceful home. I understood that now. I became more protective of them and less tolerant of Mike's behaviour. The kids became my focus, and keeping them safe became my mission.

The boundaries were an essential part of our recovery at this point. He knew it too. He completely understood and respected them. The kids and I couldn't watch him self-destruct anymore, so we agreed he couldn't stay at the house on the days he was struggling. He had a safe place lined up. We were all still in intense therapy due to the impact of all we had been through.

During his good days, love letters were still waiting for me, reassuring me that we were still *us*. Those familiar love notes always reminded me that we could, and would, get back on track and return to the normal version of ourselves. We both missed and craved the easy days.

My heart breaks when I reread the last letter he wrote. It was a letter of pure love and vulnerability. He was scared because he didn't know what more he had to do to get his thoughts under control. He told me he didn't blame me if I left him, and he expected me to. He was sad that he kept letting the kids and me down, and he didn't want his son to turn out like him or his daughter to date a man like him. This completely shattered my heart, because I knew who he was. The fact that he could still articulate the effect of all these twists and turns showed me that he was aware and therefore would be able to recover himself. He was still the man with the huge heart I fell in love with. But after reading this letter, he seemed so . . . deflated.

I just didn't know what to do for him anymore. I didn't know what he needed. He was in therapy and had an excellent medical team. I prayed it was just going to take more time. Time and discipline and self-control. Time for new patterns. Time for his brain to rewire and get back on track. Time. I honestly thought our family would return to a more recognizable version of ourselves. But he began spending less time at home, which meant he was having more and more bad days. I was learning to be okay with giving him space and time to find himself.

CHAPTER 23
SHATTERED

Mike began getting tattoos about a year after we returned from Maui. He filled his arms with images of the grim reaper, skulls, and clocks. Part of me thought it was sexy, as I had bugged him for years to get tattoos, always have had a thing for them. But I realized that it was something about the pain that was drawing him in. The kids were always excited to see his latest ink, but something about him seemed hollow. The light behind his eyes was dimmed, and his laugh didn't seem genuine. Something was different.

    I noticed he would lie on the floor with the dog for long periods of time. He enjoyed cuddling our 100 lb Rottweiler. I thought the dog was therapy for him. But there were other aspects of his behaviour that began standing out to me. Like when I was having a nap, I woke up to see him hovering directly over me - just standing there, staring at me. He was expressionless. I was startled, but he just turned and walked away. Afterwards, I heard him downstairs laughing with the kids. I never asked him about it because it made me feel really unsettled. I didn't even want to acknowledge that it had happened.

I was still making my candles and art, and I launched my company and made the website live on the Friday of Thanksgiving weekend. It was the day before our daughter's birthday. People were going to be able to see these little creations I had made. Mike was super excited for me and so proud. He enjoyed the creative process of this hobby and the fact that it had become an actual branded business. He was my sounding board for the majority of my decisions at this point.

Mike was proud of my website launch, but I could tell he seemed to be struggling. My intuition was right. He didn't partake in much that weekend. He spent very little time at home but said he would try and be at all the dinners and sports events the kids had. He didn't show up for anything. I spoke to him several times, and he reassured me that he had things under control. I chose to believe him, but I had a lot of uneasy anxiety that weekend.

The following Tuesday, as I was getting ready to leave for work, I had a powerful desire to call him. This was unusual, especially before work, as there was always a lot going on. I wanted to hear his voice and to my relief, he sounded so happy. He was driving to meet a colleague, and we chatted for about twenty minutes. He told me he loved me and to have a good day and that we'd talk later. He said he was feeling way better and had just needed space over the weekend. He told me he probably wouldn't make it to hockey practice that evening but that he'd keep me in the loop.

The kids and I went about our busy day, always hectic after a long weekend. Later that night, after hockey, the kids and I watched the last episode of our Netflix show. When it was over, I turned the TV off and tucked them in.

I crawled into my cozy bed and slowly drifted off to sleep. A few hours later, I heard a knock on the door. I woke and lay there still, thinking someone must have the wrong house. But the intrusive knocking continued. It was very strong and persistent. I checked my phone. Nothing. No unread message or text. I kept thinking that was weird because anyone needing to get hold of me would text or call me first.

I began to feel uneasy as the knocking persisted, so I brought both kids into my bed. Mike wasn't at home, and I was worried it might be him, and there was a chance this could be an unpredictable encounter. Although we had spoken earlier that day, I hadn't seen him since before the Thanksgiving weekend. I texted him. But there was no reply. I called him. No answer. I had a very unsettled feeling. I texted his brother, who was a city police officer, and asked if he was out patrolling and, if so, could he drive by our house, as someone was at my door. I felt silly messaging him, as I thought I was overreacting.

His brother called me immediately. He was frantic, and his voice sounded different. Fast. Panicked. Emotional. Yet he was composed. Very clearly, he told me to answer my door because police officers were waiting, and they needed to talk to me. Mike did not make it through the night.

"Huh? No. OhhhhhhhMyyyyyyGoddddd! Noooooo!"

I kept screeching those words as the adrenaline coursed through my body. I catapulted down the stairs. My stomach became engulfed with a pit of dread, as I understood there was only one reason for police officers to be knocking on my door. This had to be a mistake. Against my own will, I forced myself to open the door, and as promised, two uniformed police officers were sitting in a vehicle, waiting for me. They saw me on the porch and began walking toward me. Looming figures dark in the shadows.

My heart was racing as they approached. I calmly told them to go away. I told them they weren't welcome here. They introduced themselves very formally and were professional. Polite. Yet I saw the pain glisten in their eyes and heard the crack in their voices. It was everything they could do to be the composed officers their job required them to be. They were struggling with their own loss as they proceeded to verify that Mike had taken his life earlier that night.

Everything stopped. All I could hear was my own heartbeat as my blood coursed through my veins.

Life as I knew it had just been shattered.

I asked them to stop. But they continued to confirm the facts of Mike's death. I saw their eyes mist as they offered their condolences. They repeated themselves to make sure I understood. I refused to let their words sink in. I let my mind take me to another place. To a time when my legs were draped over Mike's and his strong hands were rubbing my feet as we talked so carefree about life.

I remember Mike telling me how awful it was to knock on a family's door and give them the news that would devastate them and change their life forever. I shook my head to remove the memory. Then I told them that Mike wouldn't do this to his family. He was trying to get better. This couldn't be happening. There had to be a mistake.

I was in complete denial as I stood there shaking my head, my arms crossed. I started rambling that they must have other calls to attend, or families to go home to. I kept talking over them as if that would stop their words. As if reminding them to go home to their families would delete this moment in time.

The kids poked their heads around the corner and asked if Dad was okay. I told them he was fine. I told them to go upstairs, which they did. The rest is a blur. People. Lights. Handshakes. Hugs. Muffins. Condolences.

Phone Calls. Questions. Coffee. Sobs. Heavy Silence. Uniforms. Tears. Doorbells.

Who brought me a coffee? Where is my husband? What is happening?

There is so much about this time that I don't remember. I was in complete shock. And denial. Mike wouldn't do this. He was my husband, and we had kids to raise. He promised me he was getting better. He knew what he had to do to stay on track. He had a sponsor now and a plan, and he promised. *He promised.* I couldn't live my life without him. I didn't want to live my life without him. We were a family. He was working on getting better. He told me that. Nothing was making sense. There was no way this was actually happening.

Then I had to tell the kids. We sat together on the sofa. First, I had to tell them that I had lied to them. Dad was not okay. I reminded the kids that Dad was sick. We talked about what his sickness looked like. We talked about how sometimes his illness made him do things he didn't want to do. Like drink and get angry. Sometimes his sickness made him sleep more, and sometimes it caused him to make poor choices. But that he loved us, which was why he tried so hard to make good choices. Like when he went to the gym and his doctor's appointments. But Dad's sickness caused him to make a really poor choice that night. I told them that Dad had had an accident in his truck. Their eyes went from fear to confusion.

"Is Dad hurt? Dad got into a car accident? Is he in the hospital? Can we go and see him?"

I then explained that Dad wasn't in the hospital because he didn't survive his accident. In my mind, I was not lying to them, because I knew Mike would never have taken his own life if he had been sober, and if he made this decision while drinking, then it really was an accident. My mind needed to believe that.

As I held my kids' hands and stared into their trusting eyes, all I could think about was the moment I changed their life. My ten-year-old son's face changed from confusion to physical pain. He looked off in the distance and let the salty tears fall as he quietly sobbed. My daughter collapsed on the floor, and her anguished howls still haunt me. I enveloped both my kids in my arms, but nothing could stop the tears. I didn't know how to console them. My babies didn't deserve this.

I couldn't breathe. I left the room. I hid around the corner, slid down the wall, and let the gut-wrenching sobs take over my body. I was lost. My kids needed me, and I just couldn't be what they needed in that moment. I felt completely disoriented. I was detached from reality. This was its own special kind of hell.

Someone else took over my parenting duties. I don't know who was there, but someone held my babies for me. I couldn't. My heart hurt too much. I couldn't look at the pain in their eyes. I didn't know how to help them because I couldn't even help myself. He completely shattered all of us that day.

The magnitude of the reality was surreal, and so many thoughts and questions ran through our minds. He knew how much we loved him and needed him. But this was final. He made it so very final. Just like that, I was a widow at thirty-seven with two traumatized children. I wanted my mom. I wanted my husband. I wanted to wake up from this fucking nightmare.

I have no idea how long I sat on the floor before the calm washed over me. I picked myself up with renewed strength and went to my kids. I wrapped my arms around them. I brought them to bed with me, and just laid with them and stared at them like I used to do when they were infants. They would drift back and forth between sleep and tears. All I could do was be there. Share space with them. Nothing was going to make this any better.

When morning arrived, there were so many people in our home, advising me what to do. The RCMP. The Commanding Officer. There was talk of media. Then the refusal of media. I nodded as if it all made sense, but my eyes were blank, and my mind was numb. There was an obituary to write. A funeral to plan. People to call. I wanted Mike buried near his mom, so Zena contacted the funeral home. I didn't know how to breathe without him, let alone plan a funeral for him.

CHAPTER 24
REGIMENTAL FUNERAL

The RCMP Chaplain was a lifesaver to me, and one of the things he helped me with was Mike's funeral. He had become quite close to Mike in the past few months, and although I was meeting him for the first time, something about him was comforting and familiar. It was as if we both understood the deeper part of Mike and spoke the same language. Mike was to have a Regimental Funeral, complete with an Honour Guard. The RCMP planned their part of the funeral, and I, with the help of friends and family, planned the rest.

I was able to see my husband at the funeral home. After arriving, I was alone with Mike in a small room. Me and him. He looked so handsome *and peaceful*. He was right there, and yet not. I pulled his shirt down and peeked at his new tattoo that was healing. I stared at his face for what felt like an eternity. The slight indent on his forehead, and the bump on his nose from an old hockey injury. The scars on his hands and face from college fights, sports injuries, and carpentry work. His fresh haircut, and the bulked-up muscles in his arms that had been so integral to his healing.

Caressing his cold face, taking in every inch of him. He looked serene. I hadn't seen his peaceful face in a long, long time. I was so angry, yet I didn't know how to be mad at him when he looked so tranquil.

Oh Mike . . . you are so loved and needed. Why did it come to this?

I wanted a slideshow at his funeral, and a couple of our friends helped me choose the photos. We started going through the photo albums and had some laughs and tears. Mike's friends and family emailed me with the ones that they loved. Thankfully, one of Mike's colleagues and a friend was a photographer, and he graciously offered to take this task off my hands. Greg helped him with the slideshow, and he asked what songs I wanted to play. I instantly knew the three I wanted.

"Picture of You," a Johnny Reid song, was chosen as a tribute to Mike's mom. Johnny Reid was Grace's favourite artist. It was important to me that I incorporate a tribute to her. "Chicken Fried" by the Zak Brown Band was the second song because it was Mike's favourite and describes him perfectly. It is a song about a man who loves the simple things in life and appreciates the small things that bring joy. I also chose Garth Brook's "The Dance," because after Mike was diagnosed with PTSD, whenever that song would come on, he told me that's how he felt about everything we'd been through. I took comfort knowing so many people were rallying together to help celebrate his life.

The morning of the funeral, I was full of denial, yet I had my morning coffee like I always did before waking the kids and getting them out of bed. They had their clothes all laid out. Family members had taken them shopping and bought them new outfits. Our son wore a black suit with a maroon shirt, and our daughter had a new black dress. I felt as if I was living in an alternate reality.

The RCMP sent a limo to pick up the kids and me, and I asked the Chaplain to ride with us. I didn't want him to leave my side. He was a rock, my dose of reality, and my reminder that we would get through this awful day. He was my safety net between the regimented RCMP and the soft side of the organization.

We arrived at the funeral home, and the kids and I were able to spend some final time alone with Mike. The kids didn't spend much time in the room as they had trouble believing that was their dad lying there. They had each written their dad a letter, and they left some special mementos with him. Once they said their final goodbyes, I had my final time with Mike. I put my head on his chest and sobbed. I was never going to see him again after this moment. I wrapped my arms around him and let my tears fall on his chest. I left wet stains all over his blue shirt. I have no idea how long I stayed like that. I didn't know how to let him go. I didn't want to live my life without him.

The RCMP Honour Guard and other Regimental Elements were all in readiness in the tiny RCMP chapel. An Elder played the drums to honor Mike's roots from Cowessess First Nation. The drums were beautiful and therapeutic. The kids and I were the last ones to walk in. Walking down that aisle felt like my wedding, except this time, I was with my kids, and Mike wasn't waiting for me with tears in his eyes.

We were escorted to the front right pew. In the left front pew, there were political leaders, police chiefs, and RCMP Commanding Officers. The Minister of Public Safety Ralph Goodale attended in his official capacity. Greg, Morgan, and their families were behind them. I remember locking eyes with each of them. Greg grabbed my hand as I walked by, and then we took our seats. The words spoken about Mike were beautiful. His friends made everyone laugh, and the slideshow made everyone cry. My kids were incredibly strong that day. I grabbed my daughter's hand as she sobbed to remind her we were going to be okay. My son was fighting back tears. I gave him a tissue, and he pushed my hand away. He told me he was fine.

The ten-minute slideshow was beautiful, and there

wasn't a dry eye. It was shocking to see our life summarized in pictures; all put together in a neat and tidy display. The silly Rider game festivities, the cozy nights at the cabin when we were snowed in, the family vacations, the Christmases full of laughter and memories. That was our life. My mind began to wander to what lay ahead for us now.

I was presented with Mike's Stetson and the Canadian Flag that had been laid on his casket. I felt nauseous. I didn't want to open my arms because I knew what it meant. I was given the final formal pieces that represented my husband's service in the RCMP. In the quiet chapel, all I could hear was my pounding heart as tears fell from my eyes. I wanted to run as far and as fast as I could. It was as if time had frozen and began again in slow motion.

This Stetson with the leather band now lay in my arms, along with my husband's heart and soul. We left the church and prepared to go to the cemetery. As the kids and I walked out of the church, my son took his dad's Stetson and placed it on his head. It was too big for him, and he looked so innocent as he wiped his eyes. The sight made me catch my breath.

Over 600 people came to Mike's funeral to honour him. It showed the impact Mike had on the police world and all the lives he touched. His funeral occurred days before our thirteenth wedding anniversary and just after our daughter's fourteenth birthday. What used to be a big week of birthdays, wedding celebrations, and Thanksgiving, is now marred by the anniversary of his suicide.

After the funeral, people I didn't even know were hugging me, many offering support. I remember thinking, where were you all when we were struggling? Did we really do that good of a job hiding it? I doubt it. But now, everyone knew our struggles and wanted to help. It almost made me mad. Why didn't you take the time to get to know him better? Did you ever ask him how he was doing? Did you ever take the time to notice the pain behind his smile? I didn't want their support now - we needed to feel safe and supported for the last three years. We had lived through hell and back as a family.

I remember some ignorant comments being made about suicide, and it stopped me in my tracks. These same people that were nowhere in sight when Mike was struggling, now had opinions? And to make matters worse, they felt they had the right to share these opinions *with me?* The stigma behind mental health and the anger and judgement of suicide is very real. But it comes from a place of ignorance. The people who passed judgment so quickly knew nothing of the man or his struggles.

Fortunately, I had many people around me that I trusted. I surrounded myself, and the kids, with people who understood our pain and confusion. As things calmed down, I began going for regular coffees with the

RCMP Chaplain, Mike's friends, and many of his colleagues. I was told that Mike had been instrumental in changing the RCMP for the better.

Mike's death was categorized as a direct result of his Operational Stress Injury (OSI), and he was one of the first RCMP Officers, who died by suicide due to an OSI, to be honored with the protocols of a Regimental Funeral. This was one, if not the first, suicide death, where the RCMP covered the total cost of the funeral and his headstone. Further acknowledgment of his death was shown by the flags lowered to half-mast at F Division Headquarters. I still remember those flags that stood at a complete standstill that day. Not a whisp of a breeze, it was an uncanny sight.

At this point, it was a well-known fact that he had been diagnosed with PTSD and had been actively processing and treating his work-related traumas in therapy for years when he lost his battle. Operational Stress Injuries were becoming more apparent within the organization, and this marked a huge steppingstone for the RCMP moving forward.

I didn't realize the full impact of this at the time. It was a giant stride for this massive organization that rarely speaks publicly of the mental health issues that plague so many of its members. That was why everyone spoke so candidly about mental health and PTSD at his funeral. It was time to shine some light on these uncomfortable topics.

As private as Mike was, I know he would be grateful that his story was used to help others. Sitting with him in Regina HQ that day when he spoke about wanting to support others walking the same path, even if that support was as simple as giving out his phone number, had been so important to Mike. He wanted people to know they weren't alone.

CHAPTER 25
THE REALITIES OF WIDOWHOOD

Some of my closest girlfriends stayed with us the week after the funeral, and we shared stories of our early days, which the kids loved hearing about. They wanted to hear more about the easy days of boating and camping and when our lives were full and vibrant. The familiar energy and support of my best friends helped take our minds off the sharp sting of the present.

Dad helped with whatever I needed, everything from paperwork to consoling the kids, to allowing for my outbursts of anger. More than anything, he constantly reassured us that we would be okay. Mike's family was around and continuously wrapped their arms around the kids and me. His college friends spent some extra time with us, and the kids loved hearing all the stories - some of which were new even to me. The kids didn't remember much about this crazy, fun-loving prankster man everyone spoke about. PTSD had changed him so much. We needed all of these people, as most had known our struggles and had been there for all of us through the years.

His police colleagues wrote their favourite stories about Mike and put them in a leather-bound book. To this day, my kids treasure that book and love reading about all the bad guys their dad caught and the office pranks and banter their dad was a part of. The stories turned their dad into a superhero. Words cannot express my gratitude that Mike is held in this regard. I witnessed his struggles daily, and for others to acknowledge that he was still regarded as a hero makes my heart smile.

There was a ton of paperwork to sign, and Zena was a lifesaver at this point. She handled all the financial and legal conversations with her clear head. She was used to dealing with wills and insurance. She truly was my brain. Zena was a godsend during this time, telling me where to sign and what to do next. She changed the meaning of what makes a fantastic friend.

That first year was a terrible time. I eventually learned I was processing what was known as traumatic grief. It was different from the grief of losing our mothers and aunt. In those cases, we had time to digest, prepare, and say goodbye. But Mike's suicide was unexpected and self-inflicted, and it came on the heels of family trauma. It was much different to process as Mike was not there to answer the many questions that arose for all of us. He created his own timeline, and it was confusing to try to process what he had been thinking while dealing with the pain. I relied on sleeping pills to get to sleep, and anxiety took over my life. We were just trying to get through day by day.

One of the most challenging things we had to cope with was knowing that everyone knew who we were. We were *that* family. I could see it in the way people looked at us, and it happened all the time. People would be across the rink, in mid-conversation, and lock eyes with me, and their faces would change into sad eyes and soft smiles. I didn't know who they were, but they clearly knew me. Spouses would corner me on football fields, trying to pick my brain about the signs and symptoms of PTSD. They were worried about their husbands. Our family now represented a cautionary tale. The worst-case scenario. I understood their panic, and now that our family problems were public, people saw me as a safe place to share their fears. I didn't mind sharing details, but I quickly learned to set boundaries.

I remember keeping Mike's phone charged on the kitchen counter during those early days. The kids and I found comfort when we would hear his familiar notifications go off. His ring tone was "Enter Sandman" by Metallica, and it was a soothing sound when the electric guitar and throbbing drumbeat would fill our kitchen. The familiarity of the sounds seemed to soften the blow that he was gone.

Life slowly continued to go on. The frustrating part was that no matter how much we put one foot in front of the other or how the kids and I seemed to be healing, there was always an unspoken heaviness that few people truly understood. Grief is so complicated. Every happy moment or memory was now tainted for our family. When something good happened, the kids wanted to tell their dad. But they couldn't. Grads, wedding days, grandkids, all these happy moments have a mark on them now. It's hard to look forward to some of these milestones. Our daughter won't have her dad walk her down the aisle. Because he was so young when his dad died, our son truly missed out on learning who his father was. He barely remembers the good years at all. Yet, I remember all the dreams Mike had for his boy. All the things he wanted to teach him; how to change a tire, how to use the tools in the workshop, how to cook a steak to perfection with the telltale grill marks. So much has been left undone.

Grief is exhausting, and it is a constant wave of ebb and flow. Sometimes predictable, but most times not. It is love that has nowhere to go - nothing tangible to attach to anymore. It is a real feeling, pockets of longing that need to be released. I would hold my kids when they cried, but it never eased their hurt. Sometimes, I would crawl into bed with them and cuddle and weep as I held their little bodies. They were my piece of Mike, but it never eased my actual pain.

On one occasion, I went to my bedroom and found my son sound asleep on my bed, wrapped in the Canadian Flag that had been draped over his father's casket. He had cried himself to sleep. I cannot even imagine the sense of abandonment my kids have felt. My son released his grief through tears. My daughter chose anger. I waffled back and forth between both, but I began writing nonstop to help process my feelings.

We were functioning and participating in life again, but we were shells of who we used to be. It's heartbreaking to see your kids smiling and laughing with their friends, but knowing below the surface is a deep pain that makes them feel helpless. That pain would show up with a vengeance behind the safety of our closed doors. The outbursts, the short tempers, the anxiety, and the lack of sleep are all real. But longing is the worst because there is no other option than to breathe and release it until it passes. It always does. You just hoped the next one wasn't going to hurt as much.

I don't think I cooked for a year after his death. I didn't want to do anything I used to do - it wasn't the same. I was a shell of myself during that first year. I was incredibly grief-stricken and knew I wouldn't have anything to give anyone if I didn't cocoon hard. No matter what I did, nothing numbed the pain. There were days I didn't get out of bed. There were days I didn't eat. There were days when I drank wine when I should have been drinking coffee. My bathtub became a staple. There were many days I was a shell of myself, going through the motions.

Those first few years of intense grief took a toll on us, and I have a lot of guilt looking back. Part of me feels guilty because my kids deserved a better childhood. After their father's suicide, my trauma and grief always seemed to interfere with the kind of mom I wanted to be. But, as time has passed, my kids reassure me that I haven't messed them up too much. There are no topics off limits with us. We talk about the good and the bad. We talk about the things we are embarrassed about, and we don't let too many issues sit under the rug for too long. I want my kids to be seen and heard by me, even when I must put my pride aside and hear some cold truths about where I've fallen short.

The kids and I did a lot of travelling the second year after Mike's death. We visited major cities in North America to visit extended family, and sometimes it was just an excuse to run. I wanted to be anywhere but home. It helped for a while, but it soon became time to deal with my fears. Beaches, Ubers, and hotel rooms can only go so far before you realize your issues are still in the suitcase and unravel like unwelcome guests whether you want them to or not. Eventually, I was able to find my feet again and was able to ground myself.

As time has passed, the ebb and flow is less dramatic now. Sometimes, we can get caught up in wishing Mike was here, but the pain has begun to lessen as acceptance began. Now when we hear "Enter Sandman," Mike's ringtone, we tell Dad to answer his phone, and when Zac Brown comes on, we dance together as a family of three.

Mike shows us he is around by the quarters and dimes he leaves for us. Quarters and dimes have a significance that makes sense to us as a family, and it just makes me shake my head in awe. My son's room is littered specifically with these coins. There will be a dime under his gaming controller or a quarter in his cleat when he dresses for football. My daughter has been known to yell at her dad to make the lights stop flickering when they turn into a strobe light in our kitchen. She texts me when she finds a dime under her makeup brush. But now, all these reminders bring smiles to our cheeks instead of tears to our eyes.

We have come to realize that we are stronger than we ever thought possible, and it has begun to change how we approach life. My kids are now quite fearless. They have come out of this tragedy as stronger versions of themselves. I have, too. Over time, there was no choice but to face the future together as we spiraled up from our cocoon.

CHAPTER 26
MOVING FORWARD

We remained in the family home for four more years. Our haunted house, as I liked to call it. The lights would flicker, the floors would creak, and coins and feathers would magically appear out of nowhere. Mike was always letting us know he was nearby. But I also still see the places in the walls where the holes used to be. What started out as an exciting new beginning for a bustling family of four and a Rottweiler now began to feel empty. The house was too big with too many memories. The house that broke me, has also given me a safe place to heal and rebuild. But it became time to let it go.

It is impossible to smell the exhaust of a snowmobile without it bringing prickly tears to my eyes. That was Mike's favourite pastime, and I used to love the smell of that exhaust mixed with the frosty air. But now, it takes me to a time and place that is too painful to revisit. I will know I am fully healed when I can walk into that stone cabin nestled in the woods and not have it bring me to my knees. Maybe one day.

Through all of this, I still miss my mom every day. And Grace. And my aunts. As I was completing this book, my mom's older sister lost her battle with breast cancer. Her cancer was not caused by the gene, but she walked a very similar path as my aunt and Mom. She would have made my mom proud at how she stepped in and was there for me and my kids over the years. The memories I have of the three sisters are nostalgic and powerful, yet I find some solace in knowing they are all together again. If I listen closely enough, I can hear their giddy laughter from the heavens, as their wine glasses clink with love.

Some of our family has fallen away, and, although that hurts, it has shown me the importance of surrounding myself with the right people. Sometimes blessings do come in disguises. My life has been full of amazing friends, and I see the world through awe and wonder now, as I navigate forward and choose people who fit.

I became more involved with holistic healing, finding comfort in Reiki, mediums, crystals, meditation, journaling, yoga, working out, and long meditative walks. I was introduced to spiritual awakening, crystals, and vibrations. Something about this drew me in, and I met people with similar interests. I see the world through a completely different lense now, and I am spiritual but no longer religious. I do not judge others and understand that we all have our own journey to walk, love to spread, and lessons to learn.

I put my health on hold for a while. When Mike died, I was in the middle of reconstructive surgeries, but I needed time to rebuild my strength. About a year later, I began the process again. I had four more surgeries in Alberta after Mike's death. I am happy that I continue to beat the odds that stole so many of my family members.

I walked away from my teaching career, and restarted Karys Layne Candles after shutting it down for a year following Mike's death. I still enjoy making candles and paintings, but they are lighter. I infuse crystals into my artwork now, and sometimes creating candles makes me sad as I think of how it all began. I'm not sure how long I'll do it for. My dad told me that if I closed it all tomorrow, I have already received abundant wealth from the healing that took place in the process. Sometimes I still allow the aromas and recipes to take me to another time and place. I'll know what I am supposed to do with the business when the time is right. Opportunities have presented themselves, and for that, I am grateful.

About a year after Mike passed away, my friend called and said a Medicine Man from New Mexico was coming to Regina and that he'd done some incredible healing work. I was always up for trying new things that would help us. I pulled the kids out of school, and we spent a whole afternoon in his healing room where sage filled the air. We sat on the floor, surrounded by smoke, knit blankets, and leather rattles, and it was peaceful and calming. He had visions dance before him that he told us about. It felt like Mike was right there.

He explained PTSD so beautifully to my kids - they developed a full understanding of how broken their father had become. He said, first of all, regardless of religion and science, people need to acknowledge they have a spiritual side. He said every time a person sees a traumatic event, a piece of their spirit breaks off and stays in that event. If people don't take the proper amount of time to heal and bring that piece back to the whole, it will remain in that event (i.e. nightmares, flashbacks, etc.). As you go from one trauma to another, leaving pieces of yourself behind - you will eventually lose who you are and lose your way.

This is where addiction and suicidal thoughts come into play. It's the after-effect of not knowing who you are anymore and what your purpose is because your spirit is so fragmented and tortured by what it has seen and experienced. The only way to bring the fragments back to the whole is to take the time to work through the trauma. It was such a beautiful explanation that helped to bring peace to the kids and me.

It's been hard being Mom and Dad, but we speak

about their dad daily. When we dream about him, we tell each other. When we have a hard day, we talk about it. When I am stopped in my tracks and can't breathe at the thought of not doing life with him because our wedding song came on the radio - I call my kids. They are my treasured pieces of Mike. They make him feel not so far away. That man has had so many tears shed for him. I just wish he knew how much we all needed him. Our family has a gaping hole that we are trying to fill with fond memories and stories that teleport us back in time.

My children will always mesmerize me with how quickly they can take me to another time and place where their father is alive and well. He would be so proud of them. I know in my heart he never meant to hurt us. We just became characters in a tragic love story. A story I choose to tell with the spirit of helping others, and bringing awareness to the importance of embracing uncomfortable topics. The biggest takeaway I have to pass on, is to be kind to one another because you don't know what you don't know.

I also went a little crazy with tattoos three years after Mike's death. First, it started with a coverup on my ankle that I extended up my leg. Then my daughter wanted matching tattoos to commemorate her dad. These tattoos for Mike now live on our wrists.

Then my hip started aching one day, and I knew what I needed to do. It was craving the pain of the needle. My biggest tattoo extends up and down my torso, and it matches my ankle with large, detailed roses and vines complete with a hummingbird to commemorate my mom. I continued with my other wrist, and then got one on my back. Every one means something, and every inch of pain held space for my healing. These tattoos reminded me of when Mike was getting his. I now understood the pain that draws you in. I found it incredibly healing, and I wear them as proudly as every scar on my body that I am no longer ashamed of.

The kids and I have been invited to various healing camps and programs over the years, including one in Ontario that is put on yearly for widows and children of First Responders. It has been a blessing to be brought into such a beautiful space with people who all speak the same language and have walked incredibly similar paths. We have gone back every year and found the friendships healing.

Then I was contacted by Wounded Warriors Canada and asked if I'd be interested participating in their inaugural Surviving Spouse Program. That week was an absolute game changer for me. It was during the pandemic when the world had stopped, and difficult emotions were surfacing again and bubbling up. I spent a week in Ontario with five widows of Fallen Officers. It was a magical time and such a sacred part of my healing journey. The ladies and I even created a candle to commemorate the experience, and we called it Coeur de la Rose - Heart of the Rose. It signifies the opening of our hearts and the healing that followed.

    I dug deep that week and let some of the topics surface that I have never spoken about publicly. I offloaded a lot of my pain in that room. I felt like an immense weight had been lifted, and it was the final piece I needed to fully know my heart was ready to move on and put the past behind me. I learned why traumatic grief was extra complicated to navigate. There was more to untangle. Traumatic grief takes over your life. It becomes an obsession with needing to know details and facts. My brain wanted to replay events, and there was desperation to understand things that I would never be able to. Learning that I was having a normal reaction to my trauma put my mind at ease, and I was able to work through it properly.

    I was given tools to help process all the facets of grief when they presented. It was sacred to be able to share such vulnerable space with others who were all walking the same path. Lifelong friendships were formed, and although it was a loss that united us, it is love and understanding that binds us. The importance of surrounding ourselves with the right people cannot be overstated.

CHAPTER 27
LESSONS FROM MY SURGERIES

There was a time when those surgeries made me hate my body, and I felt like I was a shell of a woman. Getting those surgeries was the hardest thing I have ever willingly chosen to do to myself. I didn't want to die from cancer in my 40s like my mom did. My kids needed me more than any of us ever realized. I never dreamed I would be the only parent they would have.

But for anyone contemplating this kind of surgery, there are some things I wish I had done differently . . .

Ask questions. Then ask more. I wish I had asked to see before and after pictures from my first doctor. I did not shop around for doctors, and I didn't know I could. I ended up going out of province to fix the problems she created. This cost me years, money, and countless surgeries.

I wish I had done better homework.

Find out who specializes in the technique you want. Do your homework on implants, or fat grafting. There are so many options, but my surgeons only presented the options they were comfortable with - to my detriment. Do your homework first to know what you are looking for in a surgeon. Then shop around if you have to.

My advice to anyone contemplating this kind of surgery is not to settle. It's your body, and although you are so much more than your body, you deserve the best treatment available.

Although these surgeries brought me to my lowest point, I discovered parts of me that are more than my physical self. I learned that I would be ok no matter what. My body is just my body. My breasts are just breasts. I am so much more as a person. I am a living, breathing soul with hopes and dreams, and many people overcome much worse physical struggles. Mine was an issue of vanity. Sounds trite, but it was a real struggle for me. I had to feel like less than a woman to remind myself of all the reasons why I *am* a woman.

My hysterectomy scars are barely visible, but I know what they represent. It was a process of accepting that our family was complete and being okay with knowing I couldn't change my mind. There's an emotional process that needs to happen, and my advice is to let that process happen. Sometimes we have to crack to let the light in, so be gentle with yourself when the emotions want to expose themselves.

Find out about the side effects of the surgery: the scars, the possible complications, medications, changes, and side effects. I notice that I feel amazing when I take my medication consistently, but if I miss a day for whatever reason, it can throw my whole week off. It takes a couple of days to become noticeable, but if I'm late or miss a dose, it will send me into an emotional tailspin. I will be weepy, my sleep will be disrupted, and my anxiety will be through the roof - for a day or two. I will get mild hot flashes and feel really foggy headed. I will just feel off. But then my body catches up and resets itself.

It was actually Mike who figured that out for me. We used to joke about our pre-planned cuddle days if I missed a dose. I plan and prepare for a slower, emotional Thursday if I miss a Monday dose. I'm gentle with myself now and take the time to slow down and honor what my emotional self needs.

Most importantly, do things that make you feel beautiful. The photoshoot I did that reclaimed my sensuality found me by accident. But it helped me see myself as the woman I used to be and didn't know I could be and feel like again.

CHAPTER 28
LESSONS ABOUT CODEPENDENCY

I can't say for sure where this comes from, but it must be something from my childhood. I'm positive about that. I don't need to understand the origin as I find it more beneficial to understand when my symptoms creep up and how to manage them. I have come so far, especially living life as a widow. I lost my crutch. I was forced to stand very firmly on my own. As someone who has spent her whole life relying on other people's opinions to determine her self-worth, being on my own has been huge for my personal growth and recovery. I have read more books than I can count and have become fascinated with learning to understand my worth regardless of what others think of me.

I've learned to trust my instincts and my inner voice. I know what I need. I know when a situation doesn't feel right. I can read the energy in the room, and I don't ignore the subtle effects I feel in my body - that tiny feeling when my stomach sinks, the second thought I pay close attention to.

I am compassionate and kind, but I won't give too much of myself anymore. I know where that line is. My kids understand and respect that their mom needs time and space to re-centre; otherwise it takes me longer to show up as my best self. They respect that, and it's teaching them to do the same. I respect when my kids set boundaries for me because setting them with your family of origin are the most difficult ones to set. If they can set them with me, then they will be just fine in their relationships.

I know what I need and don't apologize or feel guilty asking for it anymore. I let people fall out of my life - family included - if my boundaries clash with their agenda. I can't stress enough the importance of finding your tribe of like-minded people. If I can't be candid and speak my truth, then we're not part of the same tribe. And that's okay. Ironically, the more comfortable I have become with setting boundaries, the less I need them. I now attract like-minded people who set, respect and honor their own boundaries. It created such a healthy fulfilling circle of people in my life.

There's something to be said for surrounding yourself with the right people. My friends have seen me as a puddle on the floor, riddled with anxiety, and they remind me that it's okay to camp there for a bit, as long as I don't live there long enough to think that's where I belong. Our feelings are there to be felt, and once allowed space, they will process and move on. It's that line of knowing when it's gone on too long, which means you need to seek extra support. There's no shame in that. That is wisdom. Knowing you need something more and seeking it out. Therapy, medication, hypnosis, etc., all have their time and place, and it's different for everyone. Taking what you need is a beautiful thing, and a gift to yourself.

I think it's about finding what works for you and being willing to be uncomfortable while you figure it out. So many people run from uncomfortable feelings, and I tend to run toward them when I sense they are bubbling up. I know the faster I give them space, the faster they feel validated and move through me.

I found my healthy outlet in making candles and painting. I never had an agenda, but I think my soul did. The creativity that comes out of me when I paint and create candles reminds me that I matter and deserve to be seen, heard, and loved ... by myself first. That was a hard lesson for me to learn. But I am so grateful for the lessons and wisdom that I've gained from all the paths I have walked. I am a different woman these days, comfortable in my skin, and fearless. I never know what my next step will be, but I always find myself on the right path.

CHAPTER 29
PTSD AWARENESS

PTSD is real. It can be sneaky. It can be subtle. It can be loud. It can be inconsistent. It can destroy relationships. But, it can also be managed and controlled, with the right supports.

I have found some solace, knowing that Mike's death shone a bright light on a topic that is often avoided. It sparked some uncomfortable, but much-needed conversations within various police forces across Canada. My wish is that police training incorporates more education on PTSD at the beginning of careers. Spouses and partners should also be involved in that. Looking back, it was easy to get caught up in the culture and patterns that were the accepted norm. This often meant that dealing with job challenges entailed sharing a bottle of booze with colleagues.

The changes I noticed in Mike were initially vague; there was no way to know these subtle changes were the beginning of a volcano about to erupt. We had not been educated about it properly. It makes my heart heavy when I think of how long we lived like that before we felt desperate enough to ask for help. We were worried about what opening up would do to Mike's career, never imagining things would end the way they did.

I wasn't confident enough to contact the upper ranks when I realized that Mike needed serious help. So, I went to his best friends and colleagues who pieced together what we needed. Looking back, I needed support. My kids needed support. But where were we supposed to go if we didn't feel safe?

The day we took Mike to RCMP HQ to be registered for treatment, Morgan took the time to read the fine print on the Relapse Agreement Contract Mike was required to sign. He refused to let Mike sign the papers unless they amended the contract. The contract stated that he could face a code of conduct and possible termination if he relapsed. That was hard to digest, especially for somebody who had come forward on their own and asked for help. He wasn't there because of misconduct or performance issues; he was there because of PTSD.

After receiving treatment and education in rehab, we learned that relapses could be part of recovery. It means something is still off and you need more support.

Mike could have suffered career punishments for trying and failing. Our instincts had been accurate. I'm so thankful Morgan took the time to read the fine print for us that day. Thankfully the organization agreed to amend it, and Mike was comfortable signing off.

After his death, some of Mike's colleagues were furious with him. Many of them struggled with PTSD too, and they were mad that he just gave up. This caused its own trauma within the RCMP family. At the end of the day, there is still a lot of stigma attached to mental health, in and out of the police force.

It is difficult to hear when people open up to me about their feelings on this. I understand the lapse in judgement of Mike's final choice and the frustration and anger that followed. But I also saw the man who was suffering near the end, and hating himself because he didn't know how many more times or ways he could apologize to the people who were his world. I know it tormented him that he couldn't be the man he wanted to be for the people he loved the most.

Of course, I still get angry with him, too, because he could have made a million better choices that day - but I know his intentions and understand his heart. I've had time to process this, and it causes me to cry tears of compassion rather than anger. I know the man he was, and his heart was beautiful, and hidden behind that tough guy exterior.

I would encourage organizations to look at the stigmas that exist within their own walls. Programs, education, support, and services can all be in place, but do their members actually feel safe enough to ask for help? The embarrassment. The shame. The guilt. The paranoia. The anxiety. These are real feelings that are experienced when the veil comes off.

The nakedness, exposure, and vulnerability that has to happen in order to get help is enough to keep many members living with their sickness. There needs to be normalization within the force - around the language, and conversations regarding mental health. Anything can look good on paper, and the policy can be in place, but if people don't feel safe enough to ask for help, then it is all for nothing.

Stigma can be strong enough to stifle the supports that are in place. There needs to be flexibility and a safety net to encourage people to be honest when they need help. To truly change the culture, members need to be taken care of from the top down. This starts with candid conversations among the upper ranks, with a language central to normalizing the human feelings that surround trauma, and how messy that can be to process properly.

First Responders see so much in their careers, things the rest of us shudder and run from. Any changes in their behaviour needs to be taken seriously, no matter how subtle. Why does this have to be stated so many times? If you're human, you feel things. When did this become a weakness to hide from? There needs to be more dialogue around this. In the workplace. In the home. In the therapist's office. We need to change our language and redefine what makes a person strong. The strongest people I know talk about their feelings because it shows they are comfortable in their own skin. It takes strength to have that kind of vulnerability, and this is where confidence grows. It shows grit and determination. It shows they have been through something difficult and come out the other side to the benefit of themselves and their loved ones. That is where true bravery lies.

PTSD BEHAVIOURS TO LOOK FOR:

Withdrawn

This can be subtle at first and build over time. It is easy to assume it is related to stress, marriage problems, or work-related. It took a long time before I realized something bigger was going on. Mike started to become distant from everyone. He didn't want to be around anybody. Family and friends included. We spent more time at home instead of socializing with friends. Visits became shorter. Mike would often be found doing something on his own; he would usually find an excuse to be on his phone, away from the crowd. He seemed to become an introvert, which was the complete opposite of the man who would spend all day helping me prepare to host friends for dinner.

Anger

I noticed a quick temper, which was different from his typical temper. It seemed inappropriate to the situation, and it came on fast. It also started happening more frequently. The outbursts began to get louder. Something that would normally be an irritation started to cause anger that didn't match the situation. In our case, the telltale sign was when a hole was punched in the wall because he was frustrated. The anger was hot and fast. It became a quick, violent temper that was also unpredictable.

Irritation

Little things seemed to be a constant irritation. There was a grumpiness or moodiness associated with this - all the time. Mike became irritated from when he woke up to when he went to bed. Sleep was often the reason behind it. He couldn't get proper rest, which affected how he engaged in life. This irritation often led to a quick temper. He was always on edge and, as a result, so were we.

Sleep Disruptions

This was a huge factor in the changes I saw. This was more noticeable because it would keep me up as well. His sleep seemed to be disrupted for some reason. Sometimes it was vivid nightmares, and sometimes it was restlessness and fits of waking up in the middle of the night. Lack of sleep magnified everything else. It began to disrupt healthy eating patterns and increase the moodiness. This made things more confusing to piece together since lack of sleep can lead to changes in personality, but the telltale sign was when the nightmares became obvious. That was when I knew there was something much bigger going on than the need for a more relaxing bedtime routine.

Anxiety

There seemed to be a lot of anxiety around things, people, and situations. The anxiety was heightened compared to the reaction that would have come years prior. Sometimes this would be articulated and acknowledged, and sometimes it would come out in other ways like irritation or anger.

Paranoia

I think this is a common trait for police officers because they see terrible things, so a level of distrust naturally forms over time. But with Mike, this became quite noticeable and not in the realm of normal. He experienced paranoia about everyone, even trusted people, which became confusing. There was the assumption that everyone was to be distrusted on some level. Mike felt like he was always being watched. He was scared that the kids and I were being watched and followed. New neighbours that moved in came under suspicion, to the point that he didn't even want to meet them. This eventually led to avoiding people and socializing.

Mood Swings

Unpredictable became normal. I never knew which way the day was going to go. There were a lot of mood swings, and they could be abrupt. I never knew what triggered the anger. The kids and I became used to walking on eggshells because we started to think it was something we were doing, or not doing, that caused the trigger.

Substance Abuse

This was not as obvious as one might think. There was a lot of secret drinking and clever use of money. It was hard to pinpoint, and it went on for a long time. Over time, he did not put much effort into hiding empty bottles. I started putting it all together. Simple things that seemed thoughtful at the time had motivation behind them, such as being poured a glass of wine, but it was actually so I couldn't smell the alcohol on his breath. Or offering to go to the store, but it was so he could make a stop at the liquor store. Everything became more obvious when the substance use got really out of hand.

By the time I began finding empty bottles, all the other symptoms were in full swing. What used to be an afternoon nap became an alcohol-induced nap that I couldn't wake him from. I started to realize that he didn't have the flu or a sensitive stomach; he was hungover. Everything started to make sense as his illness progressed. I never knew I had to be a detective in my own home, so it took me longer to figure this out.

Memory Issues

I noticed I often had to remind Mike of a conversation we had had or promises/commitments he had made. I noticed, in general, that he seemed more forgetful. I sometimes wonder if this was because he kept saying he didn't know how to shut his brain off. It was as if his brain didn't want to retain any more than it had to. Because I couldn't always rely on him, this would often lead to fights.

Guilt and Shame

Mike felt so awful about how he was behaving. The guilt and shame of it was something he could never shake. He knew he wasn't this person, and he was embarrassed and felt incredibly guilty for what his kids had seen. He told me that time and again. He didn't want to act the way he did, and the frustration of not feeling in control took him to dark places. He loved us immensely and yet understood I needed to set boundaries for our safety and peace. He could often be found with his head in his hands and tears of desperation in his eyes. This vision of him, time and time again, is what takes me to a deep place of grief and longing for the man I fell in love with and lost. He truly didn't understand why he couldn't regain control of his mind and body, and I saw how it fractured his spirit.

CHAPTER 30
FINAL THOUGHTS

Mike will always be my first love, maybe my only love. Time will tell. My heart aches out of pure love for the man I lost and the suffering he endured due to the stigma of all he went through. I hold nothing but love and compassion for him. He was so much more than his illness; he truly was an amazing man. I wanted to capture the essence of Mike, and the incredible man he was. I wrote this as a tribute to him and our children.

    I hope our story will encourage others dealing with similar issues to begin the difficult and uncomfortable conversations that can lead to healing and recovery. There is healing on the other side of the pain. Everything I have been through has taught me lessons about myself and humanity in general. We need to create safe spaces for each other.

Stigma in society, and especially in police forces, is incredibly real. Public awareness, fundraisers, and education are just the start. Real and honest conversations between people is what leads to healing. I spent too many years hiding behind pretty decor and fake smiles, and I have lost too much to the shame of mental health. No family should have to suffer in silence. Speaking our truth, feeling safe enough to say we are having a shitty day, an emotional day, a heavy day, week, month, or season is what is really going to be what removes that stigma. We need to relate to each other on more than superficial levels.

People need people, and we need to feel connected, and accepted. But to be fully seen and understood, we have to get better at being vulnerable. It takes a brave person to wear their heart on their sleeve and expose their emotions to others, but there needs to be the creation of a safe space to do so.

I have come a long way from the sorrowful woman who became an extension of her candle-lit bathtub. I now choose to surround myself with people who make me laugh and make me want to experience the joys of life again. I no longer feel guilt for wanting to live and be happy. This is known as survivor guilt, and it is a real thing and something I have also had to work through.

Opening up to others can be incredibly difficult,

but every time someone takes that brave step, it helps break down the walls that keeps us hidden with our pain. Please know you are not alone in the uncomfortable emotions that you feel. Be brave, and find your tribe.

Life is short, and it is meant to be lived. I have spent enough time in the dark, damp mess of this cocoon called grief. It's time for this Gemini butterfly to spread her wings as she moves on to the next unknown chapter of her life. Somewhere near the snow-capped mountains. It's both exciting and scary, and yet I know I have the most amazing angels guiding me every step of the way.

FINDING MY FIRE

RESOURCES

PTSD / Mental Health Supports

Support for Operational Stress Injury (SOSI) Program: https://www.rcmp-grc.gc.ca/en/family-corner/support-operational-stress-injury-program?re

VAC Assistance Program: www.veterans.gc.ca/eng/contact/talk-to-a-professional

Royal Canadian Legion: www.legion.ca/support-for-veterans/mental-health-ptsd

List of RMCP Chaplains: www.rcmpva.org/chaplains

Canadian Institute for Public Safety Research and Treatment (CIPSIRT) www.cipsrt-icrtsp.ca

Edgewood Treatment Centre www.edgewoodhealthnetwork.com

Crisis Services Canada 1-833-456-4566

Canadian Association for Suicide Prevention   1-613-702-4446

American Veteran's Crisis Line 1-800-273-8255

TEMA Foundation www.tema.foundation

Wounded Warriors Canada www.woundedwarriors.ca

Canadian Critical Incident Stress Foundation www.ccisf.info

Codependency

Codependent No More by Melodie Beattie

The Language of Letting Go by Melodie Beattie

Widowhood

Widows Wear Stilettos by Caroline Brody Fleet

Camp Faces www.campfaces.org

Tips For New Widows www.TAPS.org

Wounded Warriors Surviving Spouse Program
https://woundedwarriors.ca/our-programs/surviving-spouses-program

Spiritual Healing

Destiny of Souls by Michael Newton

You Can Heal Your Life by Louise Hay

Signs: The Secret Language of the Universe by Laura Lynne Jackson

The Crystal Bible by Judy Hall

BRCA Resources

Centres for Disease Control and Prevention:https://www.cdc.gov/cancer/breast/young_women/bringyourbrave

Angelina Jolie's Article: https://www.nytimes.com/2015/03/24/opinion/angelina-jolie-pitt-diary-of-a-surgery.html

Real Self: Realself.com

FINDING MY FIRE

FINDING MY FIRE

ABOUT THE AUTHOR

Sheri Lux completed her Bachelor of Arts Degree in English, as well as her Bachelor of Education at the University of Saskatchewan. She is a former teacher, who now focuses her attention on her company; Karys Layne Candles, where she creates beacons of light to remind others to take time for themselves. Sheri continues to create crystal infused artwork, which can also be found on her website. She is also a strong advocate for mental health awareness, focusing on the signs and symptoms of PTSD within the First Responder communities across Canada. Sheri resides in Calgary, Alberta where she continues to raise her two children.

FINDING MY FIRE

www.ingramcontent.com/pod-product-compliance
Lightning Source LLC
Chambersburg PA
CBHW030035100526
44590CB00011B/215